MW01043572

My New York
A Life in the City

William J. Dean

New York, New York

My New York: A Life in the City
Copyright © 2013 by William J. Dean.

All rights reserved.

ISBN 978-1482734690

Cover photo:
Andreas Feininger/Time & Life Pictures/Getty Images
The Manhattan & Brooklyn Bridges, 1946

About the Author

William J. Dean was born, raised, educated (college excepted), and continues to work and live in New York City.

As a lawyer, he has been deeply involved in the life of the city, serving as executive director of Volunteers of Legal Service, an organization providing pro bono civil legal services to benefit poor people in New York City.

As a volunteer, he has served as chairman of the Correctional Association of New York, a civic organization with statutory authority to visit and report on conditions in New York State prisons; as chairman of The New York Society Library, the oldest library in the city, founded in 1754; as the Wednesday night driver for the Coalition for the Homeless food van for thirteen years; and as a legal adviser to the Greenmarkets in New York City. For two decades, he conducted a forum series at the New School's Center for New York City Affairs, "New York: Problem City in Search of Solutions."

Hundreds of his personal essays on a wide range of subjects have been published.

In 2011 he was the recipient of the Brooke Russell Astor Award presented by The New York Public Library, an award honoring a person "who is relentless in his or her dedication to the City and who has contributed substantially to its enrichment."

Preface

During a productive period of unemployment in 1975, I wrote a book with a friend, "The Pedestrian Revolution: Streets Without Cars" (Vintage). This gave me a confidence about writing I never had had before.

Once you start writing, it is not easy to stop. Over the past 38 years, I have written 400 personal essays. In a spirit of independence, I have never sought advance approval from an editor. I choose the subject, write the essay and then find a home for it.

Many of my essays have appeared on the "Home Forum Page" of "The Christian Science Monitor" and in the "New York Law Journal". Others on the Op-Ed pages of 'The New York Times", "Wall Street Journal", "Newsday" and "International Herald Tribune".

My annual income from writing has rarely exceeded a few hundred dollars. (Mother provided sound advice when suggesting I attend law school.) Yet the pleasure these essays have given me, both in the writing and publication, has been enormous.

For this collection, I have selected 83 essays. Topics include:

Walking, Central Park, Grand Central Terminal
Basketball and Opera
Rikers Island and Potter's Field
Bridges, Rivers, the Harbor
Whitman and Thoreau in New York
New York and Venice

These essays, and others, reflect my close ties to New York, the city forever a part of me.

William J. Dean
New York City

Table of Contents

WALKING

The City My Feet Know Perfectly

Each day I walk in the city. What Concord, Mass., was to Thoreau, New York City is to me.

The streets inform and entertain. It's hard to be lonely in a place with so much human activity. They bind me to my city. Like Thoreau, I am blessed with a strong sense of place.

New York's streets define the city. Its vitality: The noon hour on Fifth Avenue produces a surging flow of humanity.

They reflect the city's diversity. From my office in SoHo, I cross Broadway to the Lower East Side, with its Italian and Chinese populations on Mulberry Street, Spanish-speakers farther east, and Poles and Ukrainians to the north. As early as the 1640s, 18 languages were spoken in colonial New Amsterdam.

They reflect its problems. The homeless. Noise. Dirt. Congestion. Pollution.

I take practical walks — on errands, to go to work — and pleasure walks — to visit my favorite places in the city. These include the old police headquarters on Centre Street with its splendid dome. The Flatiron Building. Grand Central Terminal. Each of the four bridges spanning the East River.

And I take nostalgic walks, from 106th Street and Fifth Avenue where I was born, to 98th and 96th Streets, where I grew up, to 73rd Street, where I now live. My life has been spent within the confines of thirty-three blocks. We New Yorkers are an island people, a parochial people.

D.H. Lawrence wrote, "That I am part of the earth my feet know perfectly." I would change "earth" to "city".

[1998]

Early Mornings in New York

My daily walk to work begins at my apartment building on East 73rd Street between Lexington and Third Avenues.

In the early morning, the sidewalks are crowded with children and adults rushing to school and office. By 8:15 a.m., depending on the season of the year, the north or south side of 72nd Street is bathed in sunlight. Unlike Londoners and Parisians, New Yorkers are fortunate to have sunlight throughout the year. By comparison, New York is a southern city, at the same latitude as Madrid.

When walking to work I chose from among four world-class routes: south along Park, Madison or Fifth Avenues, or through Central Park. Most days I go through the park. This serves as one of my infrequent encounters with nature, living as I do in the heart of a great city.

What vision the city's leaders had over a century ago when they created Central Park. In the spring and summer, "so fresh and charming the grass, the blossoms and flowers." (Good Friday morning described in "Parsifal".) At Easter, the cherry trees and daffodils on Pilgrim Hill at 72nd Street are in full bloom.

After the fallen leaves of autumn comes winter, when the ground is frozen and covered with snow; never enough for me. I love snow. The city is at its quietest and most beautiful after a snowfall.

From the park I see the Frick mansion. Behind shuttered French windows hang Mr. Frick's collection of paintings: the sun-lit Umbrian hills of Giovanni Bellini. Constable country. The London of Gainsborough and Turner. The French country-side of Corot. The Netherlands of Cuyp, Rembrandt, Vermeer.

At the Central Park Zoo, I bid a hearty good morning to the California sea lions who frolic in the water, and pass the old pony track, long since shut-down, where, as children, my sister and I would be taken for rides.

The park ends at Grand Army Plaza, graced by the Metropolitan Club, the Sherry-Netherland Hotel, Bergdorf Goodman and the Plaza Hotel.

At this point I go underground and board the downtown N or R subway to travel four miles to Canal Street. The elegance of Fifth Avenue yields to the seediness of Canal Street.

TriBeCa is close by. I enter my building on Varick Street next to the police horse stable.

My workday has yet to begin, but already I have experienced many delights of urban life. To paraphrase

Samuel Johnson on London: When a man is tired of his city, he is tired of life. [1992]

A Doughnut and Art to Start the Day

My weekday breakfasts in New York are very public, consumed on the way to work along Fifth Avenue at East 70th Street at the Richard Morris Hunt Memorial fronting the Frick mansion.

In all seasons, I plunk myself down on the stone bench forming part of the monument and read the newspaper while eating a doughnut and drinking coffee, purchased for $1.50 from a street cart on Madison Avenue.

Who is this Richard Morris Hunt in whose company I breakfast five times weekly? Research on my part seems in order.

His dates: 1827-1895. He was an architect, today best known for designing the Fifth Avenue facade to the Metropolitan Museum of Art. He designed mansions for the city's wealthiest families — none of his Manhattan mansions survive — and the Lenox Library, also gone, one of three libraries later to form the founding collection of the New York Public Library.

The monument has a bust of Hunt sculpted by Daniel Chester French of Lincoln Memorial fame.

A pleasure of my "breakfast room" is gazing across Fifth Avenue at the former Lenox Library site, now occupied by the Frick mansion housing the Frick Collection. Note the use of the word "Collection." The Frick is no mere museum with art objects gathered over the years by scores of curators. Basically, it is the vision of one collector, Henry Clay Frick, a Pittsburgh coal magnate. In spring, the blooming magnolia and cherry trees in the Frick garden are a glorious sight.

By the monument, passersby stumble over a bulge in the sidewalk caused by the wandering roots of an elm tree.

Only on the coldest and wettest days of the year do I breakfast elsewhere, retreating to the protected steps of the Frick Art Reference Library on East 71st Street.

I have chosen an excellent way to begin the workday, not by milling about crowded rush-hour platforms of the Lexington Avenue subway, but with an outdoor breakfast in the company of elm trees and an architectural masterpiece.

Invigorated by nature and art, I set out for my office.

[2006]

Walking Warmly Through a City Winter

On very cold mornings in New York City, I wear my warmest suit, a heavy sweater, a long wool scarf, gloves and an old winter coat. Galoshes protect my shoes from the slush. For headgear, I put aside my elegant Borsalino and wear a knitted cap to keep my ears warm. On top of the cap I plunk a fur hat.

In New York we are walkers, whatever the weather. (In summer, on the hottest days, the tar roadway is softened by the heat.) I am now ready to join fellow residents on the city's streets. They too have abandoned elegant outerwear for warm clothing gathered from the deepest recesses of apartment closets. With faces partially concealed by scarves to ward off Artic winds, we resemble wandering bands of desperados. "Stand and deliver!" I expect to hear from a passerby.

Athleticism is useful, broad-jumping in particular, as I leap from curb to roadway, and vice versa, when crossing slush-filled streets.

By the time I reach the subway station, almost a mile away, my fingers are numb. It is not easy to manage the turnstile. I stand on the frigid platform. The subway arrives, the doors open, and I enter a car. I welcome the warmth of its interior with a broad smile. My reading glasses fog up.

I survey the bundled-up passengers in their winter costumes. Some are from the Caribbean. As the subway speeds underground through a dark tunnel, they may recall with heavy hearts scenes from earlier in their lives; perhaps palm trees swaying gently under a tropical sun.

But winter has more to offer than physical discomfort. On my way to this same subway station, I go through Central Park, passing snow-covered meadows with ice crystals glinting in the sun like diamonds. The wooden park benches have snow as their sole occupant. Dogs, let off their leashes, dance in the snow.

And at night my bedroom is brightened by the moonlight reflected on the adjoining snow-covered rooftops. From the windows I watch winter clouds pass over city streets on their way to the lonely sea. [2000]

New York City's Animal Kingdom, Wild and Tame

This morning, outside my apartment building, I see a husky that looks newly arrived from the Artic, a poodle and an English bulldog. Dogs on the street come in different sizes, shapes and colors, just like New Yorkers.

I sit on a Central Park bench to glance at the newspaper and eat a doughnut. A squirrel rushes by with a large dog in pursuit. Small in size, a park resident and city property, the squirrel deserves a defender. As a squirrel-lover and city tax- payer, I volunteer for the job.

I rise and shoo the dog away. Having lost his prey, the dog gives me a baleful glance, goes to the bench where I have been sitting and, with a single gulp, downs my doughnut. Both dog and owner flee the scene.

Continuing my walk, I pass under the Delacorte Clock at the northern entrance of the zoo. On the hour and half-hour, monkeys strike a bell with hammers and then animals circle the clock: an elephant playing an accordion, a hippopotamus violinist, a bear with a tambourine, a goat playing pipes, a penguin with a drum and a kangaroo blowing a horn along with the baby kangaroo in her pouch.

In the zoo I see polar bears swimming. Three sea lions, after savoring their breakfast of raw fish, glide through the water in contentment, or drape themselves on rocks to snooze in the sun.

I pass a herd of antelope carved in stone on the façade of a zoo building and two long-tailed iron monkeys on a gate.

In Grand Army Plaza, under flowering pear trees, I come upon carriage horses munching oats from their feed bag.

At the subway entrance at 60th Street and Fifth Avenue, I descend thirty steps to reach the token booth. On the tile walls of the station are depicted a family of playful monkeys and flock of high-flying birds. To me, they represent New Yorkers on the move, bursting with energy, ready to begin the new day.

Personally, I identify more with other wall depictions: seven turtles and a family of snails. Early in the morning, like them, I move slowly.

On the train platform wall, more polar bears, but this time in stone.

Encounters with the animal kingdom on my walk from home to subway.

[2002]

Postscript:

And in the evening, Fafner the dragon — the wheezing sound of tractors at work on the Second Avenue subway construction site.

Savoring the City, Street by Street

In his poem "My Country," the Russian poet Mikhail Lermontov (1814-1841) writes:

> These things I love, and cannot tell you why.
> Rivers in flood like seas,
> Deep in her woods the swaying of the trees,
> In the cold fields her silence — I love these.

My loves are urban and less dramatic, like the walk home after attending an evening concert at Carnegie Hall.

I leave the magnificent hall and walk to Central Park South. This is one of my favorite streets in New York. Elegant hotels with the flags of many nations flying. Horse-drawn carriages at the curb. The most European street in the city.

I enjoy Grand Army Plaza at 59th Street and Fifth Avenue, with its fine Augustus Saint-Gaudens equestrian statue of General Sherman led in triumph by the winged figure of Victory. He fondly gazes at the figure of Pomona, goddess of abundance, his companion across the plaza, atop the Pulitzer Fountain.

I walk north along Fifth Avenue on the park side beneath the branches of glorious American elms. The elegant trees stretch ahead as far as the eye can see. The fragrance of grass and trees, and at the Children's Zoo, goats, with their own distinct aroma. Leaves fall. Few people are about at this time of night.

Between Park and Lexington Avenues at 73rd Street, I savor the scent emanating from wood-burning fireplaces in the brownstones on both sides of the street.

My evening walk brings to mind a favorite passage from Vladimir Nabokov. As a young man living in exile following the Russian Revolution, he wrote, "My happiness is a kind of challenge.... I carry proudly my ineffable happiness. My happiness will remain in the moist reflection of a street-lamp, in the cautious bend of stone steps that descend into the canal's black waters, in the smiles of a dancing couple, in everything with which God so generously surrounds human loneliness." [2001]

A Symphony of City Sounds

The sounds of New York City are both harsh and melodious.

Beneath my second-floor office window in SoHo, fire engines and police cars, sirens screaming, attempt to move in streets blocked by traffic.

"Is your building on fire?" a long-distance caller asks me. "Nope," I respond, "life in NYC."

On subway platforms, passing express trains roar and arriving trains screech as brakes are applied. Waiting passengers on the platform place hands over their ears. We are fit subjects for Edvard Munch.

Huge trucks pass with horns more appropriate for the Kansas plains than the congested streets of a densely populated city. My eardrums throb from the blasts.

Garbage trucks grind away early in the morning and late at night.

Street-digging is a favorite New York activity. Each day, workers with pneumatic drills fan out across the city to repair water and gas mains and replace telephone and electric cables. They rip open the same streets over and over again.

But not all the sounds of the city are harsh.

From my apartment, located on a side street midway between two busy avenues, I listen to the singing of birds in brownstone gardens.

I enjoy hearing ship whistles from the East River, for me a reminder that I live on an island off the North American continent.

Other city sounds. On sidewalks, conversations and laughter. In subway stations, the haunting music of the Andes performed by Peruvians. In parks and squares, splashing water of fountains.

In the opera houses and concert halls of New York City can be heard in a single week the music of Verdi, Puccini, Rossini, Debussy, Wagner, Mozart, Bizet, Rameau, Donizetti, Beethoven, Bach, Copland, Ellington, Stravinsky, Franck, Shostakovich, Liszt, Satie, Poulenc, Haydn, Rachmaninoff, Sibelius, Strauss, Britten, Chopin, Schubert.

The sounds of New York: the best and worst of city life.

[2000]

In Stride with Thoreau

"I think that I cannot preserve my health and spirits," Thoreau wrote in his essay, "Walking", "unless I spend four hours a day at least — and it is commonly more than that — sauntering through the woods and over the hills and fields, absolutely free from all worldly engagements."

Thoreau could walk for miles without going by any house or crossing any road. Buildings and streets are an integral part of my walks.

Thoreau did not walk for exercise. That could be achieved, he believed, by the swinging of dumbbells. Walking for him was an enterprise and adventure, an opportunity to ruminate, to go on inner journeys, to immerse himself in nature, to "go in search of the springs of life."

My weekday walks are less cosmic. They convey me to worldly engagements, provide exercise, and allow me time to muse about the day's events.

On weekends, my walks are solely for pleasure. When sauntering through the woods, Thoreau could be stopped dead in his tracks by the sight of a pine tree. ("I love the whole race of pines.") Man-made sights have the same impact on me: the Flatiron Building and the graceful stainless-steel spire of the Chrysler Building gleaming in the sun; the grandeur of the New York Public Library and the General Post Office at 34th Street; the magnificent bridges linking the islands of the city to each other, and to the North American continent.

Walking with his "long ungainly Indian-like stride," Thoreau carried with him, as Emerson noted, "an old music book to press plants; in his pocket his diary and pencil, a spyglass for birds, microscope, jackknife and twine." My baggage is more attuned to city life: newspapers and a briefcase containing legal papers.

We both have trouble keeping our shoelaces tied. He solved the problem at age 36 by changing his lace-tying technique from a plain granny knot to a square knot. My slipknots continue to unravel.

I spend a lot on shoe leather, for the city's paved sidewalks, as Thoreau noted in 1843, while living on Staten Island for seven months serving as tutor to Emerson's nephew, provide "no give to the foot," unlike a leaf-strewn forest path.

Thoreau was unhappy in New York City. Sitting on Staten Island, this antagonist of cities arranged sprigs of white cedar in a scrapbook. They reminded him of pines that overhung the river in his beloved Concord.

When he did walk in New York, he saw things I see today. Newly arrived immigrants; in his case, "Norwegians who carry their old-fashioned farming tools to the west with them...." He saw crowds and traffic. Had he stood on a corner at Lower Broadway, he could have seen Walt Whitman passing in a horse-drawn omnibus, perhaps declaiming Homer at the top of his lungs. But the energy, noise and excitement of city life held no appeal for him, while Whitman reveled in it.

Under the influence of Thoreau, I try to be aware of nature in the city. The seasonal changes of the trees I see from my bedroom window. Moving clouds. The rivers and bays, reminders of the city's seaport origins. Along Park Avenue, tulips in spring and spruce trees at Christmas. Freshly fallen snow.

"I have traveled a good deal in Concord," Thoreau wrote. He never tired of these excursions, forever finding new things to see. For me it is the same. My city is a source of daily discovery.

Wherever he went, Thoreau carried Concord in his heart. He was, in Emerson's words, one of those who stick "fast where they were, like an axis of the Earth."

I share his strong sense of place. This year, on the eve of my 50th birthday, I traveled the geographic confines of my life, walking from 73rd Street to 106th Street. Unlike most in mobile America, I am rooted to a single place, like someone from the Middle Ages who never left his village.

Thoreau would understand and approve. [1987]

Manhattan's Straight Streets

Joseph Brodsky, in his essay, "A Guide to a Renamed City," writes of Peter the Great and St. Petersburg, the city he founded: "Carpenter and navigator, this ruler used only one instrument while designing his city: a ruler."

In their 1811 plan laying out Manhattan's streets from the city's northern edge — roughly Houston Street — uptown to the village of Harlem, the state-appointed Commissioners of Streets and Roads in the City of New York embraced the same planning principle as Peter: They drew straight lines.

Public officials in the early 19th century felt the need to plan for the city's growth. "They looked at the patchwork of street grids that then made up the City and saw the folly of allowing such a random pattern to extend the length of Manhattan," writes Morrison H. Heckscher, chairman of the American Wing at the Metropolitan Museum of Art, in a museum publication.

John Randel, Jr. acted as secretary and surveyor to the three commissioners. "Almost daily," in his words, he would go "from the city to our office, then in the country, at the northeast corner of Christopher and Herring Streets, previous to performing field work in the suburbs of the city." He encountered hostility from property owners and squatters and thick woods "impassable without the aid of an ax." Randel worked "with a view to ascertain the most eligible grounds for the intended streets and avenues, with reference to sites least obstructed by rocks, precipices, steep grades, and other obstacles."

But "by the time he'd finished [his survey] in the fall of 1810," Edwin G. Burrows and Mike Wallace note in "Gotham, a History of New York City to 1898", "the commissioners had settled on an overlay pattern that brooked no such obstacles." Influenced by the work of the Erie Canal Commission, "their vision of the streets of Manhattan had much in common with their vision of a great canal plowing across the state." Soulmates indeed of Peter the Great!

The commissioners made the most important planning decision in the city's history, creating, in Mr. Heckscher's words, an "inexorable grid that has defined the City ever since: 12 north-south avenues, all 100 feet wide, and 155 east-west streets, 15 to be the width of avenues and 140 to be 60 feet wide." They also created four avenues east of First Avenue, running north-south: A, B, C and D.

In a report accompanying their survey, the commissioners explained that they chose a rectangular plan because cities are "composed principally of the habitations of men, and that strait-sided, and right-angled houses are the most cheap to build, and the most convenient to live in."

To forestall criticism that their plan provided too little space "for the benefit of fresh air and the consequent preservation of health," the commissioners argued that "if the City of New York were destined to stand on the side of a small stream, such as the Seine or the Thames, a great number of ample spaces might be needful; but those large arms of sea which embrace Manhattan Island, render its situation, in regard to health and pleasure, as well as to convenience of commerce, peculiarly felicitous...."

The commissioners explain why they stopped at 155th Street: "To some it may be a matter of surprise, that the whole Island has not been laid out as a City; to others, it may be a subject of merriment, that the Commissioners have provided space for a greater population than is collected at any spot on this side of China.... [I]t is improbable, that (for centuries to come) the grounds north of Harlem Flat will be covered with houses."

Chancellor Justice James Kent was not alone in thinking that the commissioners had done a splendid job.

Writing in 1915, the historian I.N. Phelps Stokes, author of "The Iconography of Manhattan Island, 1498-1909", strongly disagreed. "As a matter of fact it destroyed most of the natural beauty and interest of the island...."

The historians Burrows and Wallace agree with Stokes on the commissioners' plan, writing: "Manhattan's ancient hills, dales, swamps, springs, streams, ponds, forests, and meadows — none would be permitted to interrupt its fearful symmetry." An early 19th century critic was equally scathing, believing that the city's leaders were "resolved to spare nothing that bears the resemblance of a rising ground.... These are men... who would have cut down the seven hills of Rome, on which are erected her triumphant monuments of beauty and magnificence and have thrown them into the Tyber [Tiber] or the Pomptine [Pontine] marshes."

But the commissioners' plan basically has withstood the test of time, with the exception of one enormous but felicitous breach: The creation of Central Park in the 1850s.

Postscript:

On a visit to the New-York Historical Society Library, I request "Item NS4 Range 00 in blue tube atop green shelves on east wall." This is the commissioners' plan, extending almost eight feet in length and over two feet in width. The library's senior conservator and a reference assistant unroll the plan with the utmost care on a large wooden table.

With enormous pleasure, and with magnifying glass in hand, I stretch over the table to examine the six joined sheets of the map. I find the southeast corner of Broome and Greene Streets, the location of my office, by 1811 an already developed part of the city and so not affected by the work of the commissioners.

Far to the north is one of their creations, the block where I live: East 73rd Street. My block, and the surrounding streets and avenues, then existed only on paper. There were no habitations, only woods and a ridge running west along 73rd Street to Sixth Avenue and east to Avenue A at 70th Street.

Avenue A on the Upper East Side? It seemed inconceivable, because the alphabet avenues are so linked in the minds of New Yorkers with the Lower East Side. But the commissioners, with rulers in hand, had drawn Avenue A from North Street (Houston) north to the East River. Then, leapfrogging over the river's waters, their Avenue A rejoins land at 51st Street and continues north to 92nd Street. As I came to learn on a walk there, the words "Ave. A" can be seen today on the façade of Public School 158 between 77th and 78th Streets, a reminder of Avenue A's uptown life, which came to an end in 1928 with the renaming of the avenue to honor World War I hero Sergeant Alvin York. And Avenue B became East End Avenue. [2008]

Directions

Peter the Great's favorite direction was said to be west. He moved his capital from Moscow to St. Petersburg, the city he founded, to secure a Russian window on the west.

Favoring no one direction, I go in all directions, though not at the same time.

From north to south, New York City measures 36 miles. From west to east, 16 miles. My life progression in New York City has been south (32 blocks) and east (three blocks).

When lying on the couch in my living room the other night, I realize for the first time that I face west. All these years, while reading and listening to music, and watching basketball and old movies on television, and imbibing gin and tonics and smoking cigars, clouds have been passing overhead, west to east, moving from land to sea.

In bed, my directions are north (head) and south (feet). The bedroom windows face north and east, providing welcome breezes in the heat of summer and bone-chilling temperatures in winter.

On my way to work each morning, I walk west to Fifth Avenue and south through Central Park. From the park I see rays of the early morning sun reflected-on the windows of West Side apartment houses.

My office in SoHo faces north and west. On sunny days in midafternoon, when sunlight embraces the granite pavements and cast-iron buildings, I can't resist leaving my desk to stroll north to Houston Street and then south back to the office along Greene Street, the sun on my face. In New York you need to seize moments like this, for tall buildings cast city streets in shadows much of the day.

When lost in a foreign city, I ask for directions. "Go north," a direction-giver may say. For a New Yorker, north means uptown. So, crossing an ancient bridge in search of a medieval cathedral, I proceed "uptown."

Losing my way along a country road, the direction-giver says, "Go south." South, for me, is downtown. I proceed "downtown" through flower-filled fields in search of a Catalan village.

I am not good at following directions, or giving directions to tourists on street corners in New York City huddled over maps like generals on maneuver. [2002]

I Am Beginning to Notice More About My Own City

I am strongly drawn to the work of the great French photographer Eugène Atget (1857-1927), for in it he reveals a heartfelt commitment to his city. His city was Paris, mine is New York. I respect a person's devotion to the place where he lives, having formed a close bond with my own city.

I have lived in New York City all my life. The streets, buildings, bridges and people are as much a part of me as my limbs. Not that I am an uncritical booster of New York. As a practicing lawyer and a person deeply involved with problems of poverty, crime and the homeless, I am more aware of the city's pathologies than most.

Atget, too, was familiar with what he called the "miseries and treasures" of his city. As one learns from the masterly four-volume series, "The Work of Atget", by John Szarkowski and Maria Morris Hambourg, Paris for him was both a private passion and a life undertaking. He chose as his lifework to photograph the art and architecture of old Paris as well as the traditional street trades of the city.

Atget began taking pictures of Paris around 1897. Within four years he had made some 1,400 photographs of the city. He was very independent and photographed only what he deemed interesting, beautiful or important. He cherished the cobblestone streets, the iron lampposts, the fountains and the sidewalks shaded by cooling trees. One of his early pictures, "Bitumiers," is an eloquent depiction of workmen laying down a new pavement. On their knees, the workmen, with tools in their hands, tenderly smooth the surface of the freshly poured macadam.

On numerous occasions he photographed the horse-drawn carriages of the city. (His father and grandfather had both been carriagemakers.) Shop windows fascinated him, especially those containing clothing-store mannequins. Atget's own image sometimes appears in the reflection of the glass window he is photographing.

His fondness for Paris expanded to little-noticed artifacts of the city — doors, for example. He filled at least four albums with pictures of doors. Other subjects that attracted his eye were wrought-iron signs, ornamental grilles and balustrades. He often began work at dawn and would continue until the last light of day. A photograph of the Rue de la Montagne-Ste.-Geneviève reveals a sidewalk still wet from an early-morning scrub. Empty metal milk cans are lined up in front of a dairy shop, the milkman not yet having arrived to collect them. A picture of the same scene taken later in the day shows the sidewalks to be dry. The milk cans are gone and the proprietors of the dairy store and adjoining shop have lowered striped awnings over the windows to shield their goods from the midmorning sun. As the authors of "The Work of Atget" point out, we are witnesses to the "unfolding of the Parisian day."

Atget enjoyed revisiting his favorite parts of the city. Repeatedly he photographed the quais of the Seine and the city's bridges, especially the Pont Neuf and Pont Marie. Once each year he would photograph a beloved spot in the Latin Quarter, an area given that name by Rabelais because of the Latin-speaking students of the University of Paris who used to fill the streets. Atget photographed the Luxembourg Gardens regularly over a period of more than a quarter-century. (When in Paris, I start each day at the Luxembourg by writing, seated on a park bench.)

On spring mornings he would take pictures of the Ile Saint-Louis, that haven of tranquility in the Seine. Viewing these photographs of wet pavement in fog, I am reminded of my walks along the Central Park side of Fifth Avenue in the mist.

After examining the loving detail of his work, I strive each day to notice more about my own city. [1985]

I've Walked the World Without Leaving Home

I do not own a car. The garage on my block now charges \$690 per month, plus an 18 3/8 percent New York City parking tax. If I must choose, I prefer occupying my apartment to living in the backseat of a garaged automobile.

And why own a car when other means of transportation are easily available in the form of subway, bus, taxi, bicycle and walking?

How pleasant it is to begin the day by exiting my apartment building and walking with vigorous strides along the street. After a night of sleep, the limbs are stretched, the mind clears for the day ahead, and the imagination is stirred by the sight of lively people and attractive store windows.

In a year, I walk about 800 miles on the streets of New York. The circumference of the globe is 24,900 miles. I cover this distance over a 31-year period. I have already circled the globe once walking on the streets of New York, and am well on my way to doing so again.

There is no walking tax in New York City and I need not worry about parking problems or traffic jams. In my life and in my city, foot-power has it over horsepower!

[2000]

CENTRAL PARK/ GRAND CENTRAL TERMINAL

Amid Skyscrapers, I Enjoy a Vast Estate

I was born in a hospital across the street from Central Park and not, as I sometimes claim, found under a mushroom there. (A portobello mushroom, being a large newborn.)

I have never owned land. Central Park is my closest tie to real estate — my all-seasons country place. Thus, when I read that Vladimir Nabokov inherited a 2,000-acre estate from his uncle prior to the Russian Revolution — not the best time nor place to be inheriting land — I thought, "That's more than twice the size of my 843 acre park!" (Tchaikovsky, by the way, in New York in 1891 to conduct the first concert ever performed at Carnegie Hall, visited the West Side apartment of music publisher Gustav Schirmer overlooking Central Park. Tchaikovsky assumed the entire park was Schirmer's private estate. And why not? Russian estates were huge — until the Revolution, that is.)

My youth was so centered on Central Park that I would argue with my sister Elinor when she claimed that Manhattan was an island. She turned out to be right, being more traveled in the city than I was and attending a school by the East River where she saw ships pass each day.

At school, we played soccer in Central Park on the East Meadow at 98th Street and Capture the Flag on a rock outcrop — metamorphic rock called Manhattan schist, said to be 450 million years old. It was here that I acquired an historical perspective, and many bruises.

Later, the 96th Street playground became the center of my outdoor activities, with its sprinkler a welcome amenity on scorching summer days. In the fall, the nearby chestnut trees produced beautiful mahogany-colored chestnuts encased in rough prickly rinds. I placed the chestnuts on the window sill in my bedroom where they remained until spring.

Before school, my dog and I would walk along the reservoir path. I continue the tradition of weekday morning walks in the park.

On weekends, I bicycle in the park past the Bethesda Fountain to the lake by the Ramble for views of Bow Bridge and landmark West Side apartment buildings, such as the Beresford, and then south past the Sheep Meadow to the Heckscher Ballfields.

Sitting in the ballfield stands, equal pleasure comes from watching the softball game and gazing at the Central Park South skyline.

In the stands, I hear music from the carousel that was moved here from Coney Island in 1951. For more than a century, the colorful hand-carved wooden horses have leapt high and proud, providing pleasure to riders of all ages.

In the early evening, as I make my way home by bicycle through the park, I pass horse-drawn carriages. Glancing down Seventh Avenue at 59th Street, I see the lights of Times Square in the distance. Central Park food vendors wait with their carts by the road to be picked up by trucks.

Another day in the park comes to an end for me.

[2005]

My Modest Investment Pays Relaxing Dividends

By purchasing a beach chair, I have saved myself hundreds of thousands of dollars. Now I have no need to buy a summer house.

On weekends, I carry the beach chair four blocks from my apartment to Fifth Avenue and 72nd Street and enter Central Park. Just inside the park is a meadow called the East Green. I open the chair and plunk myself down. This beats leaning against the rough bark of East Green trees, which I had done for years.

I take off my sneakers and socks. Here, with my bare feet in the cool grass, I write and read — a veritable Lord of the Manor — and watch New Yorkers at play and squirrels posing for tourists. (In a city of performers, park squirrels are no exception.)

New Yorkers live physically confining lives in small apartments and share crowded sidewalks, subways and buses. We need the park to stretch and unwind.

The views from my beach chair are splendid: a meadow, park trees and the façades of luxury apartment buildings along Fifth Avenue.

Owning a beach chair instead of a summer house means no mortgage, no leaking roof, no entertaining of demanding weekend guests, no packing and unpacking of bags. Not having a house, I have no need for a car, another huge savings.

Weekdays, I return home from work around 7 p.m., the same hour the park closes to cars. On summer evenings, I like to ride my bicycle. Entering the park from the steaming streets, I experience a welcome temperature drop of several degrees and the aroma of grass and trees.

Softball games are ending. Players depart. I lie down in the empty outfield: soft, cool grass after a day spent on hard, hot pavements and subway platforms.

I gaze at the towering Central Park South skyline. Behind West Side apartment buildings, the sun descends.

I rise from the field, mount my bicycle and resume riding. Near the Sheep Meadow, I hear the music of Verdi. Opera is being performed in the park tonight.

Darkness falls. Fireflies appear. With lights flashing on my bicycle, I join the fireflies. [2001]

Cycling Through the Centuries on a Bike

Purchasing a bicycle is not a decision lightly taken by a New Yorker. Deprived of attic, basement and garage, we cram our possessions into closets. Opening a closet door can be a life-threatening experience. The bathtub is a possibility for the bicycle, but it has other uses.

I decide to keep my new bicycle in the living room. Of beautiful design, the bike enhances the room. At Christmas I place cards on the frame and a wreath on the handlebars.

Nighttime in the city. I am on my way to a friend's apartment for dinner. I can walk, take a bus or taxi, hop on a subway, or go by bicycle. I choose the last.

I enter Central Park at 72nd Street and Fifth Avenue. The air is bracing. I bicycle past Pilgrim Hill. The cypress trees there stand like sentinels in the night. The sky is clear and the moon bright.

At the top of a steep hill I reach the obelisk. Commissioned by Thutmose III, the greatest of the pharaohs, who ruled Egypt from 1501 to 1447 BC, it took 38 days to transport by ship from Alexandria to New York in 1879, and 112 days to move by specially constructed railway from the Hudson River landing at 96th Street to this site.

Across from the obelisk stands the Metropolitan Museum of Art, brightly lit and crowded with Saturday-evening visitors. Visible from the park is the museum's Temple of Dendur.

Two additional minutes on my bicycle convey me from ancient Egypt to the 20th century in the form of Frank Lloyd Wright's Guggenheim Museum. It too is a beehive of nighttime activity.

I continue north, a white light flashing on the handlebars and a red flashing

How pleased I am to have come by bicycle. I have seen the moon, breathed deeply the park's fresh air, gazed at works of art millennia apart, and witnessed the vibrancy of the city's cultural life. My mode of transportation has transformed a routine trip into an adventure. [1998]

Birdwatching

I join friends on a bird walk in New York City's Central Park. I wish birds did not rise so early.

Prior to meeting my friends, I sit on a park bench to have breakfast. I share a cinnamon doughnut with two sparrows. Later I come to learn that sparrows came to America as stowaways on ships from Europe.

We meet at 81st Street and Central Park West. Our leader points to the sky. Flying high above the Beresford, one of the most elegant apartment houses in the city, is a great egret, followed by a herring gull.

With joggers and dog walkers, we enter Central Park at Hunters' Gate on West 81st Street. The sky is dark and threatening, with a chilly north wind; not conducive, I am told, to good birdwatching. It is a south wind that brings migratory birds from southern climes to Central Park, where they find refuge.

I am an expert on observing life on city streets. Not so when it comes to observing birds. "See the red-winged blackbird in the tree!" says our leader. I do not, as I fumble with my binoculars. A tree branch moves, but no bird. It has flown away. A Baltimore oriole goes behind a tree trunk, eluding me. I spot something yellow in the bushes. It is not a bird, but a passing bicyclist wearing a yellow jersey. Among birdwatchers, I am not enhancing my reputation.

By the lake in the Ramble, I do see a great egret standing on a rock, with a black-crowned night heron nearby. A mallard and ten ducklings swim by. On Turtle Pond, south of the Great Lawn, beneath Belvedere Castle, I see Canada geese: a mother, father and six goslings.

We encounter other birdwatcher groups. One reports spotting a yellow bellied flycatcher. I search for it. Gone. But I do see a nesting robin, a male cardinal on a fence and a red-breasted robin in the meadow.

My colleagues spot an array of birds: a magnolia warbler, common grackle, cedar waxwing, American redstart, red-bellied woodpecker, northern water thrush, northern flicker and common yellowthroat.

I hear them but do not see them.

Over the centuries, New Yorkers have come to the city from 180 lands. By comparison, the number of bird species passing through Central Park in a single year is about two hundred.

After two hours, I head for the subway and my office. I am not a success at birdwatching, but I have learned something of bird life — as I should, for we are neighbors, sharing life in the city together. [2003]

Considering Time, and Time Well Spent

On a Sunday afternoon, enjoying the luxury of free time but not wanting to waste a minute of it, I enter Central

Park. I sit on a park bench and look at notes compiled from books I have read.

"My time is worth nothing," Chekhov writes in a letter. How wrong he is! There are few writers whose time was more valuable. Think of his extraordinary talent, his immense literary output, his brief life.

He is my favorite writer. I read and reread his short stories and plays. In a letter, written to Alexei Suvorin, his publisher and friend, he explains that neither time nor money — "I never have any money anyway" — are impediments to his traveling from Moscow, thousands of miles across Russia, to the penal colony on Sakhalin Island to conduct a census of prisoners. He spends months there. The book he writes on the experience influenced prison reform in Russia.

Johann Sebastian Bach also used his time well. He composed, rehearsed and performed church cantatas, all between one Sunday and the next, week after week.

Critical to novelist R.K. Narayan was selecting the right time to begin his literary career. In "My Days" he writes: "On a certain day in September, selected by my grandmother for its auspiciousness, I bought an exercise book and wrote the first line of a novel. As I sat in a room nibbling my pen and wondering what to write, Malgudi with its little railroad station swam into view, all ready-made…."

His novels are set in the fictional South Indian town of Malgudi. Several years ago, I had the pleasure of meeting Narayan at his home in Madras, the vibrant real-life city where he lived.

Robert Lowell's reflection on writing and time: "How often it takes the ache away, takes time away…."

Father Zosima in Dostoevsky's "The Brothers Karamazov" found that with the passage of years, his favorite time of day changed. "I bless the sun's rising each day and my heart sings to it as before, but now I love its setting even more, its long slanting rays, and with them quiet, mild, tender memories."

Late afternoon. The golden rays of the sun embrace the limestone facades of Fifth Avenue buildings. I leave the park and cross the avenue to visit the Frick Collection.

After viewing the paintings, I come upon an exhibition of clocks. Some are over 300 years old, made by clockmakers when Bach lived. I set my pocket watch by one of them.

The passage of time helps place events in perspective. From "Natural History" magazine comes the concluding lines of an essay, "Sunset on the World Trade Center" by astrophysicist Neil deGrasse Tyson, director of the Hayden Planetarium: "New York City's twin towers have lost the Sun forever. But I take comfort in knowing that the Sun will rise again each day, as it has a trillion times before."

[2002]

Celebrating the Season With Songs of All Kinds

My alarm clock goes off at 6:45 a.m. I lie in bed motionless.

Silence. And then I hear the songs of birds in the gardens beneath my bedroom window. Have I awakened them? What an awesome responsibility.

It is a good day to rise early. Spring in New York City. There is not a minute to lose.

On my block, the Calgary pear trees are in full bloom, providing a white canopy of blossoms above the sidewalk.

In Central Park, I walk under blooming cherry and crab apple trees.

We should celebrate the renewal of spring in song.

In 17th century Netherlands, Dutch crews handed out songbooks to passengers boarding long-distance boats. Passengers and crews sang on the voyage. Why not give out songbooks at park entrances?

The Czech composer Leos Janácek set the street sounds of Prague to music. Central Park deserves a Janácek. Or a Puccini, who, in "Tosca", musically portrays the bells of Rome.

In the evening, I ride my bicycle on Fifth Avenue. I stop for a red light. Next to me is a car. The driver is playing Beethoven's Ninth Symphony.

The light changes. I keep up with the car for a block before losing it. How I would have liked to hear the concluding movement.

To begin my day with the songs of birds. To end my day with Beethoven. [2001]

A Lifetime at Grand Central

Julian Green writes, "There is scarcely a corner of Paris that is not haunted with memories for me." And so it is for me with New York City.

When you have lived in a city a long time, its fabric becomes a part of your life: the bridges, avenues, buildings.

One of the great buildings of New York City is Grand Central Terminal. It was the starting point for my first journey outside New York City — the beginning of all my travels. My mother, sister and I were in a taxicab proceeding south along Vanderbilt Avenue. At 43rd Street, the cab pulled into the driveway leading to the west entrance of the terminal. A porter took our bags and we entered.

From the top of the landing I saw the magnificent interior of the terminal, sheathed in marble. We walked down the stairway to the information booth in the center of the main concourse. There we inquired as to the track number for the *New York Central Railroad* train for Chicago. Thus we began our adventurous 3,000-mile train trip across the United States from New York to San Francisco.

During college I passed through Grand Central Terminal on my departures for Boston on trains with splendid names such as the *Merchants Limited, Yankee Clipper* and *Mayflower*.

In the 1980s my relationship with Grand Central Terminal changed from traveler to volunteer. I worked in a Coalition for the Homeless evening project to provide food to homeless New Yorkers, started during a bitterly cold winter, just after two women had died in the terminal.

My colleague and I would cross the magnificent main concourse, with its 75-foot-high windows and ceiling decorated with constellations of the zodiac. Beneath the Kodak display, an immense photograph of rice terraces in the Philippines, lay several huddled heaps, men napping on the marble floor. Human misery in the midst of architectural splendor. We offered each person food. "Thanks," they said, or silently nodded in appreciation. "Take care," we responded. In such encounters, conversations tend to be brief.

By Track 24, where each day the Adirondack departed for Montreal, a woman sat by all her possessions. Cautiously, she accepted food we offered.

Some people had taken refuge in telephone booths where they found a measure of safety from the dangers of the night. I saw them through the glass, huddled next to silent telephones, trying to sleep. We tapped on the glass gently, as if knocking at the door of a private dwelling. A head rose, the folding door was opened a crack, and a hand extended to take food.

Continuing our rounds, we came to the main waiting room. Here the wooden benches were filled with homeless, hungry people. They gathered around us as we distributed food. A pregnant woman asked for seconds on milk. A man lay on a bench, his trousers pulled up, revealing his badly swollen, blackened legs. At his request, we placed food by his side.

In another hour or so, when the station closes, the homeless and hungry New Yorkers at Grand Central Terminal will pick themselves off the concourse marble floor, leave the telephone booths and relinquish the wooden benches.

Some may go to city shelters for the remainder of the night, while others seek out a doorway to await the arrival of dawn.

Many years have passed since my work as a volunteer in the project. Now each time I walk through Grand Central Terminal on my way to a meeting, or home, I spend a moment reveling in the beauty of this great interior space and recall the role, tinged with joy and sadness, that Grand Central Terminal has played in my life. [1993]

Stargazing in Grand Central Terminal

In New York City, it is not easy to see stars.

The moon, yes. A fine sight is a full moon framed by buildings on the street where I live. At night, coming home to a dark apartment, moonlight fills the rooms.

But my vibrant city teems with such energy round the clock, producing so much light of its own, that distant, far brighter stars cannot compete. They are drowned out.

Astronomers like to place their observatories at dark locations. Forget New York City, with its "Great White Way" of Broadway. With the Empire State, Chrysler, and Woolworth buildings illuminated at night. With the massive bridges festooned with lights. With the less dramatic wattage emitted by living-room lamps of millions of apartment dwellers. With the headlights of vehicles traveling the city's 6,400 miles of streets.

Even over Central Park, the night sky is ablaze, not with the brightness of celestial bodies, but with the light of city dwellers.

For stars, I go to Grand Central Terminal and gaze at the sky ceiling, not light years away, but a mere 125 feet above the main concourse. Sixty are illuminated by electric lights of varying intensity to emulate the twinkling of stars. In this depiction of a daytime and nighttime winter and spring sky, ten constellations appear.

These are my stars. I don't mind that the proper order of the constellations is reversed, a mistake noticed by an astute commuter soon after the terminal's opening in 1913.

One day, business takes me to City Hall, to the main reading room of the New York Public Library at 42nd Street and Fifth Avenue, and to Grand Central Terminal. I think to myself, how fortunate I am to experience these three magnificent structures in the course of a day. On this occasion, as on all my visits to the terminal, I pause to gaze at the sky.

In the country, beneath the real sky, my knowledge of stars does not extend beyond identifying the Big Dipper. But gazing at the sky ceiling, I am able to point out Orion brandishing his club, and other constellations, to anyone passing by.

Astronomers may shake their heads in dismay, but I enjoy talking about my stars. [2000]

Subway Notes

On my way to work, I limp to the 68th Street subway station, the result of a basketball injury to my leg the night before. There I board the number 6 Lexington Avenue downtown local train. It being the morning rush hour, the subway car is jammed with people. At the 51st Street station I feel unwell. As the subway nears Grand Central, I faint.

Never before have I had an impact on the lives of so many people, for by the simple act of fainting, I bring the downtown East Side subway system to a standstill. On account of me, tens of thousands of New Yorkers arrive late for work, some making use of my frailty to justify their chronic lateness.

There is an advantage to being packed in a subway car like a sardine in a can: When you faint, you land on your fellow passengers, not a hard floor. (I wish at this time to convey my deep thanks to the passengers who broke my fall, whether voluntarily or not, who then, after performing this good deed, went silently on their way with no expectation of reward or recognition.)

When I regain consciousness, I am flat on my back in the subway car at the Grand Central stop surrounded by helpers: two police officers, each with a large German shepherd looking down on me in puzzlement, more attuned to seeking out drugs and explosives than assisting passengers in distress; two Metropolitan Transportation Authority officials; and an Emergency Medical Services team from the Fire Department who move me from the now empty subway car to the platform and place an oxygen mask on my face. (In addition to disrupting subway service, I am costing the city and state a bundle of money, with personnel from two city and one state agency tending to me.)

The platform teems with unhappy people caught up in the massive delay. The EMS officers place me in a wheelchair and carry me up a jam-packed flight of stairs, through a gate by the turnstiles and into an elevator that takes us to a 42nd Street entrance to Grand Central Terminal.

I know every inch of this area through my devotion to the terminal, a place where the spirit soars, where above the main concourse, the winged horse Pegasus, inspirer of poets, dwells as a constellation, an inspiration to every writer — poet or not — who passes beneath. (On my key ring I carry a metal tag with this depiction of Pegasus.)

The EMS team wheels me along busy 42nd Street to a waiting ambulance. We travel down Park Avenue. Through the window of the ambulance door, I see the southern façade of Grand Central Terminal, with its clock and arched windows, crowned by the messenger Mercury, with his broad brim travelling hat, winged sandals and staff received from Apollo himself.

I have always wanted to travel in a vehicle with a siren. To my surprise, the siren sound inside the ambulance is muted. People on the street, not hospital-bound patients, are the ones who go into acoustic shock when ambulances, sirens blaring, speed by.

In the emergency room at New York University Medical Center I receive prompt and considerate care from the medical team. Tests are performed: heart, blood pressure, X-ray. The tests establish that I have not suffered a heart attack, but the doctor wants me to remain at the hospital overnight. I decline. Four hours is long enough.

The hospital doctor telephones my internist. From the hospital I go by cab to my doctor's office at East 71st Street. More tests. Everything seems fine. The doctors think my fainting is "a fluke." I believe it to be linked to trauma from the basketball injury where I badly bruised my right leg going for a rebound, severely straining both a hamstring and calf muscle.

After leaving the doctor's office in midafternoon, I return to the 68th Street station and board the subway in my second attempt of the day to get to the office. At

Grand Central, the subway door opens at the exact spot where I had lain six hours earlier. I resolve that I will never again complain about delays — indeed, I will even offer assistance — when next I am on a subway and the conductor announces, "We are delayed because of a sick passenger." [2011]

MOTHER/FATHER

Mother

Mother was born in St. Petersburg, Russia, in 1903. Her father had traveled extensively in the United States, where he acquired a mastery of English to such a degree that toward the end of his eight-year stay he worked as a courtroom stenographer. He was imaginative and energetic. His knowledge of English helped him immensely in business, later enabling him to represent British and American companies in Russia, among them the Gillette Safety Razor Company in Boston.

My grandmother was a talented, high-spirited woman who assisted grandfather in business. A gifted linguist as well, she translated English books into Russian, including Barrie's "Peter Pan".

As conditions in the city deteriorated — for in 1917 Russia was both at war with Germany and in the midst of revolution — grandfather moved his family to Finland, then a duchy of the Russian empire, where he owned a summer house on the Gulf of Finland.

The house, previously owned by an American, had a library filled with books by Dickens, Trollope, Thackeray and Scott. These mother devoured, for she loved reading.

Mother's last glimpse of St. Petersburg, its name now changed to Petrograd, was when her father bought her by train from Finland to take the end-of-school-year examinations, as she and her sister and brother regularly did, to test their progress in the studies they undertook at home under the direction of tutors.

Then came the harsh realities of civil war. The house in Finland shook to its very foundations as Reds and Whites exchanged artillery fire. Grandmother hid food from marauding soldiers in the house-high snow in the garden and concealed money and jewelry in flowerpots.

Grandfather decided that mother's further education, she being the eldest of the three children, could not proceed under such strife-torn conditions, and so he arranged to send her to the United States where his business colleagues could assist her. She traveled on a Nansen passport. (Fridtjof Nansen, a Norwegian explorer and diplomat, served as the High Commissioner for Refugees for the League of Nations, with authority to issue passports to stateless persons.)

Mother arrived in Boston at age sixteen in the autumn of 1919, having traveled alone by ship from Copenhagen. She enrolled in a secretarial school in Boston and then went to work at the State House for the parole board. The top right-hand drawer of her desk contained a revolver for subduing unruly parolees. Fortunately for mother, her colleagues and the parolees, use of the revolver never became necessary. Typewriting aside, manual dexterity was not one of her strengths.

During this period William E. Nickerson, an officer of the Gillette Safety Razor Company, proposed to mother that Gillette underwrite the cost of her college education, her father being of such value to the company, having introduced the Gillette razor into the Russian army.

Mother joyously accepted this generous offer. Her enthusiasm, however, was not shared by the Radcliffe

College admissions office, for she had no documents to establish her academic credentials, these records being in Petrograd and inaccessible. After considerable persuasion by Gillette, Radcliffe relented and allowed her to enter.

Actually, she had had a superb education in Russia and was leagues ahead of most of her fellow students. Mother was trilingual, being fluent in Russian, French and English. She found it amazing that in a class on modern European history, when the professor referred to Giuseppe Mazzini, the student next to her leaned over to ask, "Who is this Mazzini?" Why, even in darkest Russia, the Italian patriot was well-known!

Mother adapted well to her new situation. She was fortunate to be young, talented, educated and resilient enough to make a new life for herself after the painful separation from both family and country.

Still, to be uprooted from one's native land leaves scars. Fifty years later, she wrote of this period: "Alone in a hospitable, but still strange land, torn away from the moorings of family life and accustomed surroundings, I suffered profoundly from an inner loneliness even while surrounded by colleagues and fellow students."

Mother chose political science for her field of concentration. As a child she experienced a persisting dream of what she would do when she grew up. She saw herself as a member of some parliament, a strange idea in czarist Russia, where the parliamentary experience was yet in its infancy. "I was standing at a rostrum," she wrote, "no doubt reconstructed in my mind from what I had heard about the English parliament from my father and some of his English friends, and delivering speeches which moved my fellow politicians to action."

This seemingly wild expectation was translated into reality in the United States, for later she often stood on platforms, not of any legislature, but at public gatherings and colleges and universities where she lectured on world affairs.

Grandfather certainly influenced her choice of study. A member of the Constitutional Democrat Party, he hoped that the relationship between czar and Duma, the representative assembly in Russia, would evolve along the lines of monarch and parliament in England. He discussed with his family the future of Russia, inculcating in his children the principle that each of them, whether girl or boy, must prepare for service to their country. He was a remarkable human being. How I wish I had known him. Alas, grandfather died in London before I was born.

Another strong influence on mother was her Russian tutor, a young woman born into an illiterate peasant family who had put herself through school and university. She was a hunchback. Mother described her as having "the radiant face of an angel, for whom higher mathematics had the beauty of music." From firsthand experience she knew of the unhappy conditions in czarist Russia. She wanted to help the poor by building dams and hospitals. In 1917 she left mother's family to join the revolution, never to be heard from again.

From time to time, mother would report to Mr. Nickerson on her progress at Radcliffe. When she expressed her embarrassment about Gillette paying her expenses, Mr. Nickerson would smile and reply, "Vera, we consider you a most promising investment."

In the final weeks of her senior year, a single hurdle stood in the way of graduation: the Radcliffe swimming test.

Unfortunately for mother, the waters of the Gulf of Finland being exceedingly cold, she had never learned to swim. Somehow the swimming instructor got her from one end of the pool to the other, perhaps by using a pole with a hook attached to her bathing suit and pulling her across. In any event, the necessary certificate was duly issued. Mother never swam again.

In June, 1925, the Russian-born Vera Micheles, reluctantly accepted by the admissions office, graduated *summa cum laude* from Radcliffe College. With continuing financial assistance from Gillette, she went on to pursue graduate studies, obtaining a master's degree at Yale and doctorate at Harvard. Eighteen years later, she was to be offered the presidency of Radcliffe College. She declined the position to pursue her chosen field of international relations at a time when the United Nations was coming into being. [1986]

A Russian Soul Rooted in New York

In an essay, Primo Levi writes: "I believe that I represent an extreme case of the sedentary person, comparable to certain mollusks, limpets, for example, which, after a brief larval stage during which they swim about freely, attach themselves to a sea rock, secrete an outer shell, and stay put for the rest of their lives."

The rock to which I have attached myself is Manhattan Island, as did my mother upon her arrival in New York City.

The life of an exile is not easy. I never appreciated the full extent of mother's losses. At age sixteen, she lost all ties to childhood friends. She lost her city, a beautiful place of canals, bridges and palaces, and her homeland.

Mother's family life was shattered. After saying farewell to her father in Copenhagen, her family eventually moved to London where he died. Her brother committed suicide in Vienna. She saw little of her mother and sister, who did not come to the United States until the late 1930s. During the remaining 53 years of her life, mother returned to Russia only for brief visits.

She lost the opportunity, living in an English-speaking land, to use her mother tongue. Among the few times I heard mother speak Russian was when at home she recited from Pushkin's "Eugene Onegin" — usually the letter-writing scene, when Tatiana declares her love for Onegin.

Russians are very emotional people. Mother had to make the difficult adjustment to an Anglo-Saxon society where "the whirlwinds of the soul natural to a Russian provoked incomprehension," as biographer Brian Boyd describes the same experience Nabokov underwent in England.

At times the whirlwinds of her soul swept over us. Discussions at home, whether family matters or politics, could become highly emotional. Once mother ordered a friend of mine out of the house because she found his political views so repellent. She slapped me when I received a low grade in Russian studies, feeling I had betrayed my heritage, and embarrassed her.

Mother did not complain of her losses. She courageously created a career for herself in the field of international relations, and even more courageously, raised two very young children.

She grew to love New York, her city by adoption, having arrived here when Harvard Law School closed its library to her — no women allowed — with the New York Public Library being the only other place where she could undertake research for her doctorate. She made certain that nothing would take her away from New York for long.

Thus, when teaching non-Western studies in a course she created at Smith College, and later, at the University of Rochester, she would go through the exhausting weekly schedule of commuting to Northhampton and Rochester on Sunday nights and returning midday on Wednesday. She endured many winter snow storms to avoid having to move from New York City.

Mother led a vibrant, successful, full life in America, but for an exile the deep sense of loss persists. I was reminded of this when reading "Chronicle in Stone" by Ismail Kadare, the distinguished Albanian writer, who describes his return from exile to the city of his childhood.

Some of Kadare's thoughts may have passed through mother's mind when she returned to St. Petersburg. He writes:

> A very long time later I came back to the gray immortal city. My feet timidly trod the spine of its stone-paved streets. They bore me up. You recognized me, you stones.... My street.... My old house.... All are gone. But at street corners, where walls join, I thought I could see some familiar lines, like human features, shadows of cheekbones and eyes. They are still there, frozen forever in stone, along with the traces left by earthquakes, winters, and human catastrophes.

Through mother's influence, I developed an abiding interest in Russian literature and history, although, alas, not mother's facility for languages. When visiting St. Petersburg for the first time, a year after her death, I responded to the city, not as a stranger, but as someone who felt he had been there before.

More than anyone else, mother advanced my education.

[1991]

Father

> David Copperfield: "I was a posthumous child. My father's eyes had closed upon the light of this world six months, when mine opened on it."

Five weeks before my eyes opened, father's eyes closed forever.

By mother's bed in our New York City apartment hung a photograph of father in military uniform. He had served in the Judge Advocate General's Department during World War I. I remember his army trunk. In the linen closet I came upon a bottle of bay rum he used as shaving lotion.

Father died of a heart attack at age 45. Having become a refugee at age 16, mother became a widow at age 33, after only seven years of marriage.

On occasion, I would be taken by mother to visit Charles C. Burlingham, a distinguished lawyer whose clients included the White Star Line, owners of the "Titanic", and a towering civic leader who played a major role in the election of Fiorello LaGuardia as mayor of New York.

Father practiced maritime law at the Burlingham firm and had been made a partner just before his death. He worked very hard, providing financial assistance to his parents, sisters and brother in Kentucky, as well as supporting his family in New York City.

CCB, as he was called, helped mother with father's burial arrangements. Father, now joined by mother, is buried in Valhalla, N.Y., not far from the Burlingham family plot and near — this pleased mother — the burial place of Rachmaninoff.

Mr. Burlingham would talk to me about father, but I retained little from these exchanges. I was very young and he was in his 80s — he lived to be 101 — and in these pre-hearing aid days, used an earhorn. Communication was not easy.

I had scraps of information about father, but in reality knew almost nothing about him. I should have pressed mother for more information, or she should have volunteered it, but she was busy earning a living to support her young family and may not have wanted to relive two happy periods in her life — childhood and marriage — marred by exile and widowhood.

A few years ago, I learned with interest of a book about to be published on Mr. Burlingham's life, "CCB: The Life and Century of Charles C. Burlingham, New York's First Citizen, 1858-1959", by George Martin. I reviewed the book for the "New York Law Journal".

And then an interesting thing happened. A former member of the Burlingham firm who had seen the review sent me a two-page memorandum prepared by a lawyer at the firm following father's death on December 3, 1936.

From the memorandum I learn for the first time the date and place of my father's birth: May 29, 1891, in Godman, Kentucky. (Albert Camus's father died in France during World War I when Camus was a young child living in Algiers. Only decades later did he learn the date of his father's birth. In his book, "The First Man", Camus concludes, with deep regret, that he can never know his father, the first man in his life.)

I learn that father attended Union University in Jackson, Tennessee. (I never heard the sound of father's voice. Did father speak with a southern accent?) Like many talented and ambitious young American southerners in the early 20th century, father came north to study, in his case, at Harvard Law School, and then to practice law in New York City.

I learn that as a lawyer father was considered by his colleagues "thorough, resourceful and tenacious, yet always fair and courteous to his opponents," and that in discussions he "displayed a liberal temper and freedom from bias."

I learn that in connection with insurance litigation involving the authenticity of paintings, father made an exhaustive study of the works of Leonardo da Vinci and other old masters, visiting European galleries and consulting art experts. Now I understood why our living room bookshelves were filled with art books, many on Leonardo.

Father had met mother in New York City at the Foreign Policy Association, where she worked after completing her university studies. The organization had been created in 1918 to inform Americans on foreign policy issues following the entry of the United States into World War I.

Father shared mother's deep interest in foreign affairs. Together they traveled extensively in Europe, studying political and economic conditions. (I do remember mother telling me that she spent part of their honeymoon sitting in cafes in Trieste reading newspapers while father attended to a maritime accident in the harbor.)

In contrast to my classmates, I had a very modern upbringing like many of today's children who live in a single-parent household with a working mother. This meant I saw far less of mother. Still, she was my greatest teacher, introducing me to an exciting, wide-ranging view of life and the world.

Though knowing very little about the legal profession, and without giving much thought to the matter, I followed in my father's footsteps, attending law school and then practicing maritime law.

It did not take long for me to realize that my contribution to the world of commerce was going to be nil; that the work I was doing went against my grain. And so I sought out, and was fortunate to find within the legal profession, positions that played to my interests and strengths.

As I look back over the years, a part of me feels shame for not having learned more about my father, the man whose name I bear,

And a part of me questions proclaiming this shame. Here, at least, I can invoke the words of Montaigne: "Many things that I would not want to tell anyone, I tell the public; and for my most secret knowledge and thoughts I send most faithful friends to a bookseller's shop."

But I have, over the past few years, come to learn more about father than I knew before. What has emerged are the outlines of an admirable human being. [2009]

A Matter of Priorities

As a widow with two young children to support, solely dependent on her own earnings, mother was forced to operate within a tight budget. Given these constraints, some of her spending priorities might be considered frivolous.

First and foremost came education. No one could challenge this. But following education came these priorities: travel, restaurants, theater.

In most respects, we lived a frugal life, renting an apartment, having no country house, and never owning a car. (Mother couldn't drive anyway.) Such modern conveniences as a dishwasher, washing machine, air conditioner, or even a television set — that is, until the start of the televised Army-McCarthy hearings — played no role in our lives.

Mother did not stint on education. My sister and I were sent to private schools in New York City. Mother ensured that we received the finest possible education, an undertaking as expensive as paying for a house, but far more lasting.

I agreed with her other priorities as well. The nature of her work, writing and lecturing on international relations, necessitated extensive travel. I was fortunate to be included as luggage-carrier on trips to Asia, Africa and Europe. The fact that my mother was Russian-born also drew her to Europe. There she could speak French, which she had spoken from childhood, and enjoy the delights of foreign travel. Delights, I must confess, to which I was totally susceptible.

We had a housekeeper during the week, but on weekends mother would have to fall back on her slender culinary skills. These consisted of broiling lamb chops, boiling frozen string beans and baking potatoes. The alternative, preferred by the three of us, was going to a restaurant. Through this enjoyable arrangement, I became familiar with the cuisines of many lands.

I remember going to one of the first Japanese restaurants to open in New York City following the end of World War II. While at college I was made to feel dissolute by my Puritan New England classmates because of my New Yorker's fondness for restaurants.

Mother loved the theater. At college she had performed in plays. Indeed, she was a theatrical person, with a sense of drama and a skill at holding an audience's close attention when she lectured.

I certainly benefited from this interest of hers. The original production of "Oklahoma!" served as my introduction to the musical theater. Not a bad way to begin! This was the golden age of the Broadway musical. "South Pacific," "The King and I," "Kiss Me, Kate," "My Fair Lady," "Candide." And also the golden age of American playwrights: Eugene O'Neill and Tennessee Williams.

Mother bequeathed no real estate, but she did provide me with a solid education and a deep appreciation for travel and culture. She opened my life to a wider world without ever making me feel less American. These intangible possessions, called "unreal estate" by Vladimir Nabokov, are a lifetime gift. [1987]

EDUCATION

Sounds of School: Bells, Songs and King's English

The ringing of a hand bell by an attendant to announce closing time at the National Gallery of Scotland in Edinburgh evokes memories of school days. At St. Bernard's School in New York City, each day began and ended this way.

Many of the teachers at school — we called them masters — were English. They were strict. Throughout the day I would respond, "Yes, sir," "No, sir." So much so, that when conversing with mother at home, at times I would call her "sir", much to her amusement. (Lest the reader think I was well-behaved and compliant, both at school and at home I responded politely before doing whatever pleased me.)

Our masters were unusual teachers. When you asked Mr. Sindall a silly question, he would start humming the National Anthem, putting an end to further inquiry. To interrupt would be both rude and unpatriotic. But when you had something worthwhile to ask, he would be helpful.

Humphrey Fry was my favorite teacher. He was tall and dignified, yet always approachable. He came to teaching somewhat late in life, having served in the British army and been a barrister. A highly educated man, he truly spoke and wrote the King's English. He could easily have taught at a university, but preferred teaching young children. How fortunate we were that he did.

He cared for our well-being, revealing this in innumerable ways: in the detailed comments he made in his neat, precise hand in the margins of the scrawled chaos that constituted our attempts at prose; in the seriousness with which he approached teaching, as if it were a noble calling, and that we, for whom the effort was being made, must therefore not be without some significance; in his kind words of encouragement following an academic setback. Even in his critical remarks. They were never cutting, but expressed in the spirit of, "We both know you can do better than this."

In the English tradition, Shakespeare was an important part of school life. We performed his plays in the seventh and eighth grades. The major roles were given to the best students. Alas, the roles assigned to me were small. In "Julius Caesar", as the soothsayer, I had one line — but an important one — warning Caesar, "Beware the ides of March." He failed to heed me, with fatal consequences. In "Macbeth", I was not even a witch.

The school had wonderful songs. On the cover of the song book was the Latin word "Concinamus" — "Let us sing together." And sing together we did, at assemblies and on every other occasion. I find myself still singing these songs.

The songs suggested a way of life to which we should aspire. Like these lines from the "School Hymn":

> And free from envy, malice, hate.
> To help the weak, the wrong to right,
> Then may we keep the Golden Rule
> For home, for country, and for School. [1999]

Blessed by Embracing Two Cultures

Early on I learned something of life's complexity. At St. Bernard's I was taught by English masters, and at home, influenced by my Francophile mother.

At school we read English poetry, performed Shakespeare's plays, ate shepherd's pie with Worcestershire sauce, played soccer, and sang with fervor "Men of Harlech."

Comrades, keep close order!
Ever they shall rue the day.
They ventured o'er the border!
Now the Saxon flees before us;
Victory's banner floateth o'er us!
Raise the loud, exulting chorus,
'Britain wins the field!'

During World War II my nightmares were not about Hitler but the Spanish Armada landing on English soil and forcing us to become Catholics.

But at St. Barnard's, I received a splendid education in the English language, both written and spoken.

At home, mother did not dislike the English — she never used the term, "perfidious Albion" — but France and Russia have historical and emotional ties, and mother was Russian-born. So excellent was her French, she lectured at the Sorbonne on international relations. I felt proud when Parisians praised her French, for she spoke, I was told, in the classical manner.

I studied English history at school. The French monarchy was not well-regarded, nor was Napoleon.

French history only became a part of my life when I visited Paris and the palaces and castles along the Loire River. Then I changed my allegiance from the English Henrys to King Henry IV of France who sought, during the Wars of Religion between Catholic and Protestant, to unite a divided people. "I am a shepherd King," Henry said, "who will not shed the blood of his sheep, but seek to bring them together with kindness."

The passage of years has led me to embrace both cultures.

Thus, when returning from Gloucester in the west of England where I had worked for the summer in a bookshop, as the train pulled into London's Paddington Station, a woman sharing the compartment leaned over to ask, "Are you in the Guards?" I smiled and departed without speaking. lest my accent betray me. This remains a high point of my life. That day I purchased a Guards tie and continued to smoke Senior Service cigarettes (from a pack of five — I couldn't afford a full pack) and carry a copy of "The Times" and an umbrella.

Around the same time I came upon Michel de Montaigne, a joy of French literature — of all literature — and Hector Berlioz's glorious opera, "Les Troyens". And also 'The Plague" by Camus, for me one of the most important books I have ever read.

Looking back, I realize there are distinct advantages in being taught by English masters and having a Francophile mother. [2002]

Baseball

Away, away to fields of play!
What is the game we play today?
The game we name is the best of all,
From breezy Spring to glowing Fall,
Our own great game of Baseball, Baseball!

Thus opens the St. Bernard's School "Baseball Song," written by Francis H. Tabor, cofounder in 1903 of the school.

I played center field on the St. Bernard's Second Team. The Second Team was comprised of the flotsam and jetsam from the First Team. My main concern was to avoid being hit, rather than hitting the ball. A baseball is a hard, solid object. Traveling at high speeds, it can inflict bodily harm. As a result, my battling average hovered close to the daily temperature.

I enjoyed playing center field. The team played on Randall's Island in the East River. Soft grass underfoot, the glorious skyline of the city, tugs tooting on the river, airplanes positioning for their approach to LaGuardia, multicolored butterflies darting about. In such a setting, one could reflect on the wonders of life and dream of great deeds to be undertaken in the future. Day-to-day hassles — Latin, homework, going to bed early — faded away.

Occasionally there were intrusions, taking the form of hysterical screaming by my teammates as the ball headed in the direction of center field. I paid little attention to these distractions. I preferred grounders to fly balls. To the coach's intense annoyance, I played so deep in center field that a ground ball would barely be moving by the time it reached me. Not being able to throw far or with any accuracy, I would run with the ball and hand it to the second baseman to do with it what he thought best.

Mr. Tabor's hymn in praise of the national pastime continues:

> A pitch, a crack, the ball flies back,
> A swift dispatch, a clever catch;
> Quicken your pace and race for base;
> You're safe! You're out!
> Oh, hear us shout at Baseball.

The big game of the season against Greenwich Academy found me as usual in center field counting cars on the Triborough Bridge and wondering when the Boston-bound train would cross the Hell Gate Bridge. A glorious spring day. Humming to myself, I nibbled fresh shoots of grass.

In the last inning, I heard an ominous sound, the sharp crack of ball and bat. Seeing the ball arch upward in the direction of center field, my situation became immediately apparent. Catching the ball would make me a hero. If I flubbed, disgrace for me and defeat for the team.

To return to the ball. With the batter rounding first, the ball reached its zenith and began a downward descent. Teammates headed toward center field to help out.

Down, down came the ball. I could do nothing to avoid it. As a self-protective measure, I placed my open glove in front of my face. Plop into the glove went the ball. Having plopped in, it decided to pop out. But before the ball hit the ground, I caught it with my bare hand. My teammates were delirious with joy.

Details of this event were recounted to me by the captain of the Second Team, now a middle-aged Wall Street baron. He tells me that he still has nightmares about my catch. I informed my captain that I have never lost a wink of sleep over the game of baseball.

But spring is generous. In that spirit I will let Mr. Tabor have the final word:

> Of Golf or Hockey take your fill,
> Play Polo, Tennis, what you will;
> Seek every sport from bower to stall,
> Nulli secundus, King of all
> Is our great game of Baseball, Baseball!

[1979]

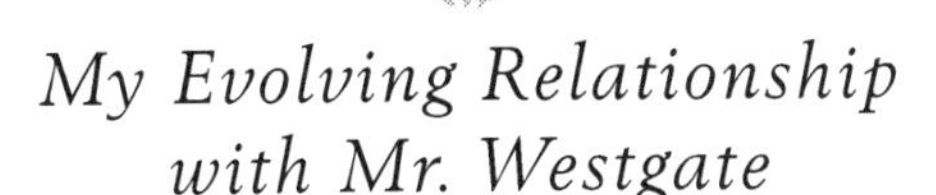

My Evolving Relationship with Mr. Westgate

I had a difficult relationship with R.I.W. Westgate, the headmaster, while a student at St. Bernard's. Once during a class, he told me that if I didn't like what he was doing, I could leave. I left and went home, copying the Russians who were walking out of sessions of the United Nations Security Council at the time. I became an instant school celebrity. Walking out on the headmaster simply wasn't done.

Another time, during a homework period, I was admiring my baseball cap. Mr. Westgate came over, took it from me, and tossed it out the window. I thought this very unfair, as did he, for a half-hour later he told me to go get the cap. I went out on the street and pretended to look for it. Pretended, because a classmate had already retrieved the cap and it was safely back in my desk.

But once I graduated from St. Bernard's, our relationship improved. Indeed, while I was a student at Columbia Law School, Mr. Westgate asked me to teach current events one afternoon a week at the school.

When I finished law school, completely out of the blue, he asked me to go to Puerto Rico to start an elementary school, where I taught for four months until the permanent head could come from England. Mr. Westgate had been requested by a trustee of the new school, a former St. Bernard's parent, for help in finding both a permanent and interim head. His offer was hugely appealing to me, for after three rigorous years of study at law school, followed by intense cramming for the bar exam, I needed time away from the law. (Reading this, I chuckle to myself. My need for time away from law, even before starting the practice of law!)

And so I became head of an elementary school in Fajardo, Puerto Rico, exchanging my nineteen-year status as a student for that of teacher and school administrator.

Following several sessions at St. Bernard's with Mr. Westgate, who explained to me what was expected of a head, and loaded down with books he gave me, I set off on my first job.

In San Juan I was met at the airport by the school-board chairman and driven directly to meet Sister Maria José. She ran the Catholic school in Fajardo and was concerned that the new school would take her best pupils. My apprehension about the meeting vanished when she opened her mouth and I heard the familiar accent of Brooklyn, U.S.A. Sister Maria José and I got along fine. We did take some of her best pupils, but were not a Protestant school. This calmed her down.

The school was located in a beautiful house, once a private residence, with a garden. The students were the children of parents working as managers at a sugar plantation, the Fajardo East Sugar Company.

Fajardo Academy opened with a student body of twenty-one, both boys and girls, and three teachers, including me. In one classroom I taught grades four through eight — eleven of the children — in all subjects but Spanish and art. My presentations on American history drew heavily on Allan Nevins and Henry Steele Commager, whose "Short History of the United States" I fortunately had taken with me, since there were no other history books. The children, ages nine through thirteen, furiously took notes as I lectured.

The school day ran from 8 a.m. to 3 p.m. I then performed administrative chores, went swimming, had supper, and returned to the school to work until 10 p.m., preparing lessons for the next day. My education philosophy was simple: Learning should be fun. Passersby on the street would hear gales of laughter issuing from the open windows of the school.

I was assisted in making learning fun by the arrival of Misty. One morning the students and I came upon an abandoned, undernourished puppy on the porch. The children named her Misty, and the school adopted her. Spoiled by all of us, Misty became quite the performer, jumping on my desk and wagging her tail to the intense delight of the students, and later, during her teething phase, nipping children, seated at their desks, at the ankle. No child dozed with Misty in the room.

Being human, at times I would be grouchy with the students, especially when they were sloppy in their work. Too grouchy, for some of the girls would cry. Having attended only all-boys schools, I was not prepared for this.

One day I had my comeuppance. A letter arrived from the New York State Board of Law Examiners notifying me that I had failed the bar exam. From that point on, I became more sympathetic to the academic difficulties of my students.

These events occurred in the fall of 1962. Mother would call at night from New York about a missile crisis in nearby Cuba. I told her I had no time to worry about such things, being too busy preparing lessons for the next day.

My inability to speak Spanish was not a major problem, since the children all were bilingual. When dealing with the woman garbage collector, who spoke only Spanish, or by telephone with education officials in San Juan who wondered who I was and what I was up to in Fajardo, I would summon the Spanish teacher, or an eighth-grader, to serve as interpreter.

Time passed quickly, too quickly. As Christmas drew near, the students bade me farewell. Tears were shed, including by me. To the tune of "The Halls of Montezuma," the students sang:

> Mr. Dean, why do you have to go?
> You have been so nice to us.
> You have taught us all we know,
> So now our brains aren't dust...

(Hmmm. I might have done more work with the children on rhyming.)

The new head arrived from England. His first official act was to banish Misty from the premises. She found a home with one of the children. I returned to New York to take the bar exam again, this time successfully, and begin my career as a lawyer.

At age twenty-five, I was a retired headmaster, a status not yet achieved by Mr. Westgate, as I delighted in pointing out to him. Through work together on the school project, our relationship had deepened. "Mr. Westgate" became "Bill," and we became friends. [2005]

Late Bloomer

At Collegiate School in New York City, perhaps the oldest school in the country, having been started by the Dutch in New Amsterdam in 1628, I held undisputed claim in the senior class academic ranking to position 17 in a class numbering 21 boys. Not promising college material.

It was believed, however, that I possessed other attributes. For example, I had prepared a lengthy report on reorganizing the school. My classmates were vastly amused by the undertaking and the school administrators charitable about the unsolicited recommendations. The only casualty of the affair was Henry Adams, a wonderful English teacher who had made books, among them Thomas Wolfe's novel, "Look Homeward, Angel", come alive for me in a way I had never before experienced. His anguish arose from the many spelling mistakes in the report. Why hadn't I shown it to him before distribution? Each misspelled word he considered a blot on his reputation.

In any event, this effort, plus other less bizarre undertakings at school, hinted at leadership skills that seemed to add a glow to a dismal academic record.

Each senior met with Wilson Parkhill, the headmaster of the school, to discuss college preferences. Mr. Parkhill stood about six-and-a-half-feet tall, but because of his personal warmth, we, his students, never found him intimidating. I told him I wanted very much to go to Harvard and could not imagine myself being happy at any other place. This happened to be true, but there were many far more talented boys in my class.

Mr. Parkhill indicated that, given my grades, this request would present him with a considerable task, but he would do his best. (Dear Reader, these events occurred in the unpressured 1950s, when close working relations existed between school headmasters and deans of admissions. Today I would be advised to consider only "safe schools." In my day, thank goodness, the term had not yet been invented.)

Mr. Parkhill performed ably. I was admitted to Harvard as a "late bloomer." The concept is admirable, recognizing that some youngsters develop slowly. I hope that a few late bloomers still manage to find their way in.

Every solution brings forth a new problem. What was to become of my dog, Penny, if I left New York City to go to college? At home, I was Penny's sole caretaker. Again, I asked Mr. Parkhill to intercede, feeling confident that he would help. He owned two dachshunds, and he and I had discussed the irresistible appeal of dogs. Mr. Parkhill undertook this assignment with more enthusiasm than the first.

But success was to elude us. The Harvard dean of admissions informed Mr. Parkhill that earlier in the century a freshman and his parrot had been admitted, and following unpardonable behavior by both, the nature of which was not divulged, both had been expelled. The result: a strict rule against students having pets.

The choice became Penny or Harvard. I chose the latter, but not without anguish. I found a home for her with a store owner on Fire Island. There she could run to her heart's content. But at college I missed her. The first month there, I spent a huge amount of time trying to locate a home for Penny in Cambridge. Eventually a telephone operator at the college agreed to take her. I sent a letter to the store owner informing him that I would be coming to reclaim my dog. He wrote me a sensible, understanding letter saying, of course, I could have Penny back, but questioning whether the plan made sense.

In fact, it made no sense whatsoever. Sanity prevailed, and not a minute too soon. Penny remained with her new master and I buckled down to my studies and immersion into a new stage of my life. [1986]

The Other Education I Got at Law School

When I arrived at Columbia Law School in New York, I was almost lecture-proof. I had been a student for too long.

At law school, I sought to penetrate the dark thickets of the law. But real property, evidence and other courses seemed very dry after the cornucopia of intellectual riches I'd been exposed to as an undergraduate.

Years after finishing law school, I came across this passage by Carlos Fuentes about his time at the law school of the National University of Mexico in Mexico City:

> When I would bitterly complain about the dryness and boredom of learning the penal or mercantile codes by heart, he [the law-school dean] would counter, 'Forget the codes. Read Dostoevsky, read Balzac. That's all you have to know about criminal or commercial law.' He also made me see that Stendhal was right that the best model for a well-structured novel is the Napoleonic Code of Civil Law.

Dostoevsky, Balzac and Stendhal enabled Fuentes to get through law school. Thomas Jefferson and John Marshall did the same for me.

In my second year, I approached the constitutional law professor Gerald Gunther and asked if I could do a paper on Jefferson and Marshall. These two men — one the principal author of the Declaration of Independence and third president of the United States, the other a chief justice of the Supreme Court — differed on the appropriate role for the federal government, with Marshall favoring a strong central government and Jefferson one far more limited.

I was granted my request.

I abandoned my basement desk in the law school library, where I was working like a dog to no useful effect, and moved to the American history room at Columbia's Butler Library. There I read every book I could find on these two remarkable men. At Butler, I was, if I may borrow a phrase from Berlioz, written while composing his opera "Les Troyens", contented and immersed "like La Fontaine's rat in his cheese."

The most important lessons I learned from my readings were: That two men of the highest intelligence and patriotism could arrive at vastly different conclusions on an issue of supreme importance. That sometimes there is more than one right answer. That life is more complex than I had ever imagined.

I found joy in my research and writing, but deadlines loom and semesters end. I completed the paper and handed it in.

In his office a few days later, Professor Gunther returned the paper to me. I fled to my basement retreat. There, in utmost privacy, expecting the worst, I turned to the last page to learn the grade: an A. I was thrilled beyond belief.

I raced back upstairs to his office and barged in without knocking. He was meeting with a colleague. He looked up in surprise.

"Professor Gunther," I blurted out, "I have never received an A from anyone." I then withdrew, lest he reconsider the grade.

Without this project I might not have finished law school. It energized me for the final lap. I started my third year with confidence and a sense of achievement, thinking that perhaps going to law school might have been the right decision after all. [2001]

LAWYER/HOMELESS/ PRISONERS

Lives Transformed: My Own and Others

Twenty-five years ago, I was sitting at my desk at a law firm, surrounded by commercial documents, wondering to myself, "What am I doing with my life?"

The telephone rang. An executive recruiter was on the telephone, pursuing a familiar ploy. "Do you know anyone who might be interested in heading a nonprofit organization?" "What does it do?" I asked. His response: "Poverty law." My response: "Yes! Me!"

Soon thereafter, I bade farewell to the world of commerce and became executive director of Volunteers of Legal Service (VOLS).

I came to the job knowing little about legal services for the poor. I had had extensive experience with nonprofit organizations, but in different fields, both as a staff member — serving as executive secretary of Citizens Union working on civic reform issues in New York City and State, and at the International Institute for Environmental Affairs, where I participated in planning events for the United Nations 1972 Stockholm Conference, the first world-gathering on environmental issues — and as a volunteer, serving as chairman of the Correctional Association of New York and the New York Society Library.

The mission of VOLS is to develop projects to provide pro bono civil legal services to benefit poor people in New York City, and then to recruit, train and mentor volunteer lawyers to undertake the needed legal services. Forty-four law firms in the city have taken the VOLS Pro Bono Pledge. In 2011, these firms reported performing a total of 1,005,201 pro bono hours — mainly providing free civil legal services to poor people in the city or to organizations assisting the poor — through participation in the projects of public interest and legal services organizations, including VOLS projects.

Poor people are most in need of civil legal services in the areas of housing, public benefits, immigration, family law and special education, each an essential of life relating to shelter, income, legal status, family relationships and the education of children.

Pro bono work provides an extraordinary opportunity for lawyers both to help those in great need and to enrich our own lives. At VOLS I relish the joys and epiphanies lawyers experience in their pro bono work. Here are examples, as shared with me by our volunteer lawyers:

- "These families are desperate to secure their basic rights to shelter, something that obviously impacts their children's ability to succeed in school. Some of our clients live under terrible conditions, with rodent infestation, cold air coming through broken window frames, open wires. The work we lawyers do is a valuable life lesson for us. We see the power of what a lawyer can accomplish...."

- A volunteer lawyer arranges with the landlord to make repairs and is present on a weekend to ensure that the repairs are properly carried out. "This was a great family. Very welcoming.... I learned that the father works on Fulton Street in a Chinese takeout place. To save money, every day he bicycles from uptown Manhattan to work. Years ago, when my own family came from Pakistan to New York, we lived in a housing project on Coney Island, so I very much identify with his family."
- A partner: "I love these cases....To hear the relief in a client's voice when we achieve a successful outcome is very rewarding....When I recruit for this project, I tell lawyers at my firm, 'Here is an opportunity for you to make a real difference in a family's life.'"
- "There is little you do as a corporate lawyer that draws you into emotional dramas. I think these cases bring out the best of your talent and skills. I worked on a housing matter with the family of a teenage boy who was very ill. This young man held the family together — a kind, mature, loving spirit. I would meet with him at the hospital. He was going through so much with his illness and the added burden of wanting to make sure his mom and dad were taken care of. Sadly, he died.... As the father of four young children myself, working on these cases means a lot to me."
- A lawyer working with incarcerated mothers on child-custody issues: "I've found my involvement with the project to be one of the most rewarding aspects of practicing law in New York. Every so often I get a call from a released mother to say thanks and let me know that she has her kids back. That is a great call to take!"

- A lawyer working with the elderly poor: "I especially enjoy working with Russian-speaking immigrant clients. They remind me of my own grandmother back in Russia: sweet, proud and vulnerable at the same time. And I try to treat each one of them as if they were my relatives and to make them feel a little more comfortable and cared for in this new country that they (and I) now call home."
- "I know that our presence in these correctional facilities serves as a beacon of hope for all the women incarcerated there. I cannot think of a more essential and fulfilling experience."
- A lawyer working with AIDS patients: "My clients remind me that wealth is not limited to dollars. Compassion, fortitude, candor, optimism and humor are equally as valuable. Those are the qualities that my clients demonstrate during our meetings, and they are qualities that I strive to emulate both professionally and personally."
- "Most people who come to us have lost their employment and sole source of income through no fault of their own. They are truly downtrodden. I knew I wanted to continue doing this work after I called one of my first clients to inform him we had won our case. My client was overcome with emotion, as it had been a huge struggle for him just to get the carfare to take the subway to the hearing. When he told me, 'You are the best thing to ever happen to me,' I knew that I had made a real difference in another person's life."

For the past quarter century, I have had the good fortune to work on legal matters that I deem to be of the highest importance and to work with lawyers who strive to fulfill the Biblical injunction in Deuteronomy, "Justice, justice shall ye pursue all the days of your life." The work has been life-transforming for the clients, for the pro bono lawyers and for me. [2011]

Scenes of a City's Grandeur and Need

On Wednesday evenings I drive the Coalition for the Homeless van through the streets of New York City. I meet my fellow volunteers at 7 p.m. at East 51st Street. We are a diverse lot: lawyer, designer, author, playwright. In the van we have containers of hot chicken-vegetable soup, bagels, milk and oranges. Enough to serve several hundred people.

We proceed down Park Avenue past St. Bartholomew's Church, the Waldorf Astoria and skyscraper corporate headquarters, turning east at 46th Street. Our first stop is at 34th Street by the East River. Here, homeless men from a nearby shelter gather each night. They are a lively group, chatting with us and among themselves. It is not too cold tonight. This encourages conversation.

We continue on our way, along the FDR Drive, past the dark swirling tidal waters of the East River. Then comes one of my favorite New York City sights, the magnificent

Manhattan and Brooklyn Bridges, side by side, spanning the East River. An "N" train travels slowly over the Manhattan Bridge toward Coney Island and the sea.

Coming off the FDR Drive, we encounter concrete barriers and trucks filled with sand to protect police headquarters, the Metropolitan Correctional Center and the United States Court House on Foley Square.

At Centre Street, in a parking lot surrounded by the three city courts serving mostly poor people — Family Court, Housing Court and Criminal Court — we provide food to homeless men and Chinese grandmothers. I call this area the Street of Sorrows.

The grandmothers live in nearby Chinatown and come to obtain food for their grandchildren. In warm weather, the grandchildren accompany them. The children's fathers likely work as waiters in Chinatown restaurants and the mothers in garment factories. The grandmothers are both caregivers and foragers. They especially want milk for their grandchildren. Tonight we have extra milk and can oblige.

We continue down Broadway past City Hall, the Woolworth Building and St. Paul's Chapel. Here George Washington came to pray following his inauguration as president at Federal Hall.

Close by, under the glare of powerful lights, is ground zero. Work continues night and day.

Our last scheduled stop is the Battery at the southern tip of Manhattan. It is always the coldest spot, with winds whipping off the harbor waters. Staten Islanders rush by to catch the ferry.

After being served, the homeless men and women return to the ferry building, where it is warm, or travel back and forth on the boats.

Across the street is a bust of Herman Melville, honoring his birthplace at number 6 Pearl Street. Melville, in his short story "Bartleby, the Scrivener," eloquently writes of the homeless Bartleby: "Immediately then the thought came sweeping across me, what miserable friendlessness and loneliness are here revealed! His poverty is great; but his solitude, how horrible!"

If food remains, we deliver it to flop houses on the Bowery. I return the van to a parking lot at 63rd Street and 11th Avenue.

New York. City of bridges. City under siege. City of rich and poor. City of joy and suffering. [2002]

I Think of David

In a preface to "David Copperfield", composed toward the end of his life, Dickens wrote, "Of all my books, I like this the best."

"David Copperfield" has been described as a passionate autobiography. Dickens, like David, knew poverty and deep loneliness early in life. His kind but improvident father landed in the Marshalsea, a debtors prison in London, for a 40 pound debt when Dickens was twelve years old. The boy would visit his father there. John Dickens told him that when entering the prison gates, he felt that the sun had set upon him forever. Dickens later wrote that his father's words broke his heart.

During his father's imprisonment, Dickens worked 12 hours each day at a shoe-blacking warehouse, hating every minute of it. He lived by himself in a boarding house, for his mother, along with the other children, had joined her husband in the Marshalesea. He felt abandoned by his family. "I know that I lounged about the streets, insufficiently and unsatisfactorily fed. I know that, but for the mercy of God, I might easily have been, for any care that was taken of me, a little robber or vagabond." Exploring London alone, he saw the wealth and poverty of the city.

As a young boy, David Copperfield, like Dickens, is forced to work. He too feels abandoned. "From Monday morning until Saturday night, I had no advice, no counsel, no encouragement, no consolation, no assistance, no support, of any kind, from any one, that I can call to mind, as I hope to go to heaven!" With hungry eyes, David would stare at the venison shop in Fleet Street and at the pineapples in the Convent Garden market. He visits the debtors prison where his friends, the Micawbers, in flight from creditors, had sought refuge.

David's anguish exceeded even that of the young Dickens, for after running away from his hateful warehouse job, he became homeless, an outcast, "against whom house-doors were locked, and house-dogs barked."

David found refuge in the country cottage of his great-aunt. As he sank in gratitude and rest upon a curtained bed with snow-white sheets, he remembered all the solitary places under the night sky where he had slept, and "prayed that I never might be houseless any more, and never might forget the houseless."

I think of David when I work on Wednesday evenings helping to feed homeless men and women in New York

City. I strive to be like young Copperfield, a person with, as Mr. Micawber put it, "a heart to feel for the distresses of his fellow-creatures when they are behind a cloud."

And, like David, never to forget the homeless. [1986]

Working at the Finest Masterworks

In an art gallery in New York City my eye is drawn to a Rembrandt etching of a beggar warming his cold hands at a chafing dish. Close by, another Rembrandt etching shows a lonely wayfarer of the road in rags.

Rembrandt produced many such etchings and drawings. At that time in Holland, beggars were a familiar sight, victims of the Thirty Years War then engulfing much of Europe, and others impoverished by personal misfortune unrelated to war.

As an artist and human being, Rembrandt felt drawn to these people. They became a lifelong interest of his, beginning with his early days in Leyden as a young artist and continuing in Amsterdam through his periods of prosperity and personal poverty.

Rembrandt was not unique in selecting beggars as subjects. The originality lay in his approach. Jacques Callot, the French artist, who was a contemporary of Rembrandt, represented beggars as comical figures, intended to amuse the viewer. Rembrandt's approach differed. As Jakob Rosenberg writes in "Rembrandt, Life & Work", "His emphasis lies on their deplorable condition, on their loneliness, exhaustion, and tragic degradation to an animal-like state."

Rembrandt's portrayal of destitute people vanquishes time and place for me. They provide a startling immediacy. The beggar warming his hands at a chafing dish in 17th century Holland is brother to the homeless man I see tonight warming his hands over a fire in a vacant lot in the city's Meatpacking District. His Amsterdam beggar in rags resembles the man I pass huddled in a doorway seeking protection from the cold.

We do not need painterly skills to see these people as Rembrandt saw them. We need only to relate to the suffering of other human beings. All who open themselves to the suffering of the destitute, and work to relieve their misery, are capable of creating their own personal masterpieces.

[1982]

Potter's Field

> And the chief priests took the silver pieces, and said, It is not lawful for to put them into the treasury, because it is the price of blood.
>
> And they took counsel, and bought with them the potter's field, to bury strangers in.
>
> — Matthew 27: 6-7

The Old Negroes' Burial Ground, north of Chambers Street, became the potter's field for the city sometime before 1755, serving as a burial place for slaves, paupers and criminals, and for American prisoners during the Revolutionary War when the British occupied the city.

For a time, Union Square and Madison Square were potter's fields. In 1797, New York City purchased the present site of Washington Square for this purpose. Fifty-seven prominent New Yorkers, among them Alexander Hamilton, strenuously objected, pointing out in a petition to the common council that the field "lies in the neighborhood of a number of Citizens who have at great expense erected dwellings on the adjacent lots for the health and accommodation of their families during the summer season, and who, if the above design be carried into execution, must either abandon their seats or submit to the disagreeable sensations arising from an unavoidable view of and close situation to a burial place...." The common council rejected the petition.

As New York expanded northward, a potter's field farther removed from the center of the city became desirable. The potter's field at Washington Square was abandoned in 1825 for a public burying ground on land lying between Fifth and Sixth Avenues, from 40th to 42nd Streets, the present site of Bryant Park and the New York Public Library. Subsequent potter's fields were situated between Fourth and Lexington Avenues, from 48th to 50th Streets, and on Randall's Island and Ward's Island.

In 1869, the city purchased Hart Island in Long Island Sound. A portion of the 100-acre island was designated as a potter's field. Louisa Van Slyke, an orphan who died alone in Charity Hospital at the age of 24, became the first person to be buried there. Since then, more than 600,000 paupers have joined her.

Hart Island continues today as the city's potter's field.

Reached by the Department of Correction ferry from City Island in the Bronx, Hart Island more resembles a New England coastal scene than a city graveyard. Fog. Buoy bells. Fishermen on their boats in yellow rain gear. Mussel shells washed ashore at high tide. Swamp grass swaying in the breeze. Wild ducks and Canada geese.

The island's scenic beauty is deceptive. Abandoned buildings, once institutions for cholera victims, prisoners and drug addicts, come into view. Building doors swing on shattered hinges. Old-fashioned iron lampposts stand blind. Bleachers removed from Ebbets Field rot in an overgrown meadow.

Dark thoughts intrude with the arrival from Manhattan of the Health and Hospitals Corporation morgue wagon. Today's delivery: each in a pine coffin; 24 adults and 29 babies. The adults range in age from 30 to 88 years. One died in a Bowery flophouse, another in the Staten Island Ferry Terminal, a third on a southbound subway at York Street in Brooklyn. The life span of the babies was from three minutes to 23 days.

The morgue wagon moves along the bumpy dirt road to the grave site for adults. The rough pine coffins are unloaded by sentenced inmates from Rikers Island. Here the living poor bury the dead poor. A prisoner writes the dead person's name on the coffin, or the word "unknown." (Once a homeless man gave me as his name, "no name.") A trench, eight feet deep and 150 feet long, has been dug to receive the coffins. They are placed in the trench in columns three boxes high. Prisoners cover the coffins with earth.

Nowhere more than on Hart Island do the living feel no envy for the dead. In place of individual headstones, a marker will be laid to identify the spot where this group of paupers is buried.

The morgue wagon proceeds to the trench for baby burials. Some of these babies were alive for too short a time to receive names. A nearby stone cross bears the legend, "He calleth his own by name." By what name are the nameless called?

For the poor, death brings no peace. After the cemetery detail of prisoners returns to Rikers Island, vandals arrive by boat. Already they have removed everything of value from the island, including the bell in the church belfry, and now they desecrate graves.

In New York City, we need police officers to protect even the dead. [1981]

The Two Worlds of Rikers Island

Everything that lives is holy. – William Blake

On Rikers Island, New York City's main jail, prisoners arrive handcuffed together. Men and women. Young and old. (Today there are 11,600 inmates on the island.) More than two-thirds of them await trial, not having been able to obtain bail. Others serve sentences of less than a year for misdemeanor convictions. Some are there awaiting parole revocation hearings.

Newly arrived prisoners, after being strip-searched, are taken to a cell or dormitory. Through barred windows some can see a nearby profusion of trees. This is the Rikers Island tree nursery. Here, under the supervision of the Department of Parks, trees, about the same number as inmates, are grown for future planting on city streets and in city parks.

The inmates on Rikers Island tend to be young, poor, minority and jobless. Far greater diversity is found in the tree nursery: London plane, Norway maple, elm, pear, cherry, honey locust, linden, ginko, weeping willow, goldenrain, pagoda, sweet gum, white ash, fir, poplar, hemlock, cedar, and black and white pine.

While inmates spend much of their time in idleness behind steel bars, locked doors and high chain-link fences, in the nursery life undergoes constant renewal.

On cold mornings, when a gray winter sky adds to the bleakness on this island of prisoners, a Parks Department gardener, as if to dispel the oppressive gloom, makes a decision to plant trees. With pruning shears, he snaps off cuttings from branch ends of existing Norway maples that show a year's growth. The six-inch cuttings are bundled together and placed in clean sand, deep enough to be afforded protection from the frost.

With the arrival of spring's beneficial warmth, the cuttings are removed from the sand and unbundled. Each cutting is inspected to determine whether a protective healing surface has formed over the wound, marking the point of separation from the tree. From the base of the cutting will develop a future tree's roots. The cuttings are taken to a propagating area and each one is planted separately in sand. Daily the cuttings receive a soft sprinkling of water similar to the refreshing mist coming off the waters of Long Island Sound. Leaves, straw or hay are matted down to help retain moisture. Rows of fully grown London plane trees provide salutary shade from the intense heat of the midday sun. Each cutting is checked from time to time to observe if roots are forming.

After a year, the growing Norway maples are removed to the nursery and placed for the first time in soil where they will stay for two years. Bamboo stakes are used to support the young trees to encourage each one to grow tall and straight. The trees receive water and fertilizer. Windbreaks in the form of privet hedges serve as a protective buffer, reducing desiccation and wind damage.

In the island's correctional facilities, inmates awaiting trial are awakened at 5:30 a.m. to begin the journey to court. Handcuffed together, they board the Department of Correction buses as the first streaks of light herald the arrival of a new day. Searched after entering the courthouse, they wait for hours in crowded court pens before making their appearances. In the evening, they arrive back at Rikers Island, are strip-searched and returned to their cells.

Meanwhile, beyond the high fences, the Norway maples continue to grow. In three years' time, the original cutting will have become a four-foot-tall tree. The young trees are ready for removal to an open field. In the fertile soil of Rikers Island, the trees will grow well over a foot every year. Even while in the field, the young trees are accorded close attention. Sentenced inmates, working under the direction of the nursery's two gardeners, prune branches and water and fertilize the trees.

After four years in the field, the Norway maples stand 12 to 15 feet tall. They are now ready to leave the protective life of the nursery for life on the outside. The months of October and November, after the trees have lost their leaves and entered a seasonal sleep, are the best time for removal from the nursery.

The care the trees have received — nourishment in the form of water and fertilizer, pruning to strengthen both the trunk and roots, protection by windbreaks and the use of stakes to keep them growing straight — vastly improves the ability of the young trees to survive the dangers of the street.

The inmate completing his sentence also prepares to leave Rikers Island. His preparation for life on the street has been less thorough. He turns in his prison clothing and boards a Department of Correction bus to be taken to Queens Plaza, 125th Street in Harlem or Jay Street in Brooklyn. Leaving the bus, he may have little more than a subway token in his pocket.

* * *

I am indebted to Robert Zappala, Parks Department gardener at Rikers Island, who patiently explained to me each wondrous stage of a tree's growth. [1984]

Fidelio's Hope, and Mine

Two deep interests of mine are prisons and opera. With Beethoven's "Fidelio", these interests converge.

The opera takes place in a prison outside Seville in 18th century Spain. The setting is a prison courtyard. Cells are seen with barred windows and iron doors shuttered with heavy bolts. In the background looms a high wall with ramparts.

The world of high walls, barred windows and locked cells, along with more recent prison paraphernalia such as fences topped with gleaming razor wire, is familiar to me in my capacity as chairman of the Correctional Association of New York, a private organization formed in 1844 and authorized by the Legislature to report on conditions in New York state prisons.

I suspect that prison sounds have not changed much since the 18th century. The loud, cold, clanging sound made when steel impacts on steel, produced by the locking and unlocking of cell doors. The shuffling of feet as prisoners march to and from their cells.

In the opera, the jailer, Rocco, comments, "Hard is the jailer's gloomy task." Life in prison continues to be hard for both the keepers and the kept. Walls and bars produce a deep sense of claustrophobia. Today's cellblocks are not the dungeons of "Fidelio", but they can still be grim. Long corridors lined with cells. Prisoners standing behind bars, silently gazing into the corridor. Others lie on their beds and stare at the ceiling.

Tensions exist between guards and prisoners and among prisoners. Yet, acts of kindness do occur. In "Fidelio", Rocco releases the prisoners from their cells to walk in the castle garden on a day when "The sun is shining/ The Spring begins to smile again." Joyfully the prisoners emerge from their dark cells into the sunlight. "Oh what delight! To breath the air,/The open air around us./Here light still comes to greet us…."

On my visits I have met correction officers who are sympathetic and understanding, and prison staff who work hard with inmates to address the problems that afflict most perpetrators of crime: poverty, lack of education and job skills, drug and alcohol addiction.

In prison, it is important not to lose hope, for the absence of hope leads to despair. Leonora, who has gained entry to the prison disguised as the young man Fidelio to try to free her imprisoned husband, realizes the need to avoid despair: "Sweet hope, oh never let your star,/Your last faint star of comfort be denied me." Even the prisoners in their dungeons cling to hope: "The voice of hope still whispers here...."

Hope is nurtured when a prisoner has loved ones on the outside who care about him. It is Leonora's devotion that sustains her imprisoned husband. "By your love," Florestan tells her, "I was protected."

I have watched inmates waiting for visitors and seen the warm smile of recognition when they arrive. "No, my family has not given up on me. I may be without a job, without a future, but still I have something." An embrace. Hand in hand, the inmate and his loved one walk to a table and begin their precious hour together. These visits, and letters from home, are a lifeline for prisoners.

Release from prison is the central concern of every inmate. In "Fidelio", the prisoners ask, "Oh freedom, will you be ours once again?" Florestan is freed to the sound of trumpets with the arrival of the king's minister. No trumpets of deliverance will sound for the inmates I meet.

Life on the outside will not be easy for the released prisoner. If prison has served as a repair shop for the inmate, a place where he has learned job skills, rather than a scrap heap that has left him no better able to function on the outside than when he entered, his chances of success are vastly enhanced.

May every person leaving prison share the aspirations of the prisoners in "Fidelio": "We shall be freed, we shall find peace."

[1986]

C.3.3

In my hands, on stack 9 of the New York Society Library, I hold an early printing of Oscar Wilde's poem, "The Ballad of Reading Gaol." C.3.3 was his cell number when a prisoner at Reading. On the title page the author is identified by cell number, not by name.

On May 25, 1895, then age 39, a jury found Wilde guilty of committing indecent acts. Within minutes of the verdict, the trial judge sentenced him to two years at hard labor. From the courthouse, he was taken to Newgate prison in London where a warrant authorizing his detention was issued, and then taken by prison van to Holloway where, "An officer noted down a minute description of his appearance, distinctive marks, color of his eyes, hair, complexion, any scars," writes Richard Ellmann in his magisterial biography, "Oscar Wilde" (1988, Alfred A. Knopf). Wilde changed from his own clothes to prison clothes, the prison rules were read to him and he was led to a cell.

Days later he was removed to Pentonville, a prison for convicted felons, where he received a medical examination. He slept on a plank bed with no mattress. "He would exercise in the open air daily for an hour, walking with the rest of his ward in Indian file, no talking being allowed."

On July 4, Wilde was transferred to Wandsworth in southwestern London. A visitor, writes Ellmann, "noted that his hands, which clasped the bars, were disfigured, their nails broken and bleeding." His face was so thin that the visitor could scarcely recognize him. Dysentery and injuries from a fall landed him in the prison infirmary for two months.

> I know not whether Laws be right,
> Or whether Laws be wrong;
> All that we know who lie in gaol
> Is that the wall is strong;
> And that each day is like a year,
> A year whose days are long.
>
> — "The Ballad of Reading Gaol"

Things were not going well for Wilde at Wandsworth, so the authorities decided to transfer him outside London to Reading Gaol in the city of Reading. Here he complained of the "thickly-muffled glass" in his cell window which allowed him no view of the sky.

> I never saw sad men who looked
> With such a wistful eye
> Upon that little tent of blue
> We prisoners called the sky,
> And at every happy cloud that passed
> In such strange freedom by.

Breaking the rule of silence when walking single file during exercise hour, prisoner C.4.8 said to him, "Oscar Wilde, I pity you because you must be suffering more than we are." Wilde almost fainted at the human sound. Without turning, he said "No, my friend, we are all suffering equally." That day, he was to tell André Gide years later, "I no longer wished to kill myself."

Ellmann writes, "It was insanity, he said, of which he was particularly terrified; the insufficiency of books, the closing-off of the world of ideas in 'this tomb for those who are not yet dead.'"

Wilde reported to a friend, "If you resist, they drive you crazy," perhaps, Ellmann writes, "in reference to the dark cell where he had probably more than once been placed and given bread and water."

With bars they blur the gracious moon,
And blind the goodly sun;
And they do well to hide their Hell,
For in it things are done
That Son of God nor son of Man
Ever should look upon!

He benefitted from the appointment of Major J.O. Nelson as governor at Reading Gaol. One of Nelson›s first acts was to go up to Wilde and say, "The Home Office has allowed you some books. Perhaps you would like to read this one; I have just been reading it myself." Ellmann writes, "Wilde melted into tears." He was provided writing materials.

Wilde's final days in prison were harrowing. He believed prisoner A.2.11 to be demented. Regarded by the doctors as a malingerer, A.2.11 was sentenced to 24 lashes. Wilde heard from the basement of the prison "revolting shrieks, or rather howls."

Three children arrived at the prison, having been convicted of snaring some rabbits. Ellmann writes: "Wilde saw them as they were waiting to be assigned to cells. He knew only too well the terror they were feeling, and the hunger they would feel." He asked a guard, "Please find out for me the...names of the children who are in for rabbits, and the amount of the fine." Wilde paid the fine, securing the release of the children.

> For they starve the little frightened child
> Till it weeps both night and day:
> And they scourge the weak, and flog the fool....

I recommend to colleagues, when we go on visits pursuant to the Correctional Association›s statutory authority to visit and report on conditions in New York State prisons, that they read Wilde›s poem, for "The Ballad of Reading Gaol" conveys many present realities of prison life. Claustrophobia; depression ("Something was dead in each of us,/ And what was dead was Hope."); harshness ("And never a human voice comes near/ To speak a gentle word."); isolation (why visits from family members are so important); mistreatment of mentally ill prisoners; the achingly slow passage of time.

But Wilde, during his time in prison, also encountered administrators and guards concerned with the welfare of prisoners, as we do on our visits to New York State prisons.

On the day of his release from prison, May 19, 1897, Wilde left for France. He began "The Leftover Years," Ellmann's moving term for the remaining 3 ½ years of his life when he lived abroad in exile, separated from his wife and two sons, shunned by many and impecunious.

He began "The Ballad of Reading Gaol" two months after his release. A prison reformer had urged Wilde to use his literary skills to make this "great subject" his own. This was to be his last literary work.

Wilde wrote of the poem, "...it is my chant de cygne, and I am sorry to leave with a cry of pain — a song of Marsyas, not a song of Apollo...."

At one time he criticized Dickens for being too preoccupied with social issues in his writing. Two years in prison had changed Wilde›s priorities.

The first six printings of "The Ballad of Reading Gaol" identified the author as C.3.3. With the seventh printing, his name was placed on the title page in brackets beside C.3.3.

He inscribed a copy of the poem to Major Nelson at Reading Gaol «from the author in recognition of many acts of kindness and gentleness.»

On Nov. 30, 1900, at age 46, Oscar Wilde died in Paris. He is buried in Père Lachaise cemetery. His monument bears an inscription from "The Ballad of Reading Gaol":

> And alien tears will fill for him
> Pity›s long-broken urn,
> For his mourners will be outcast men,
> And outcasts always mourn.

[2012]

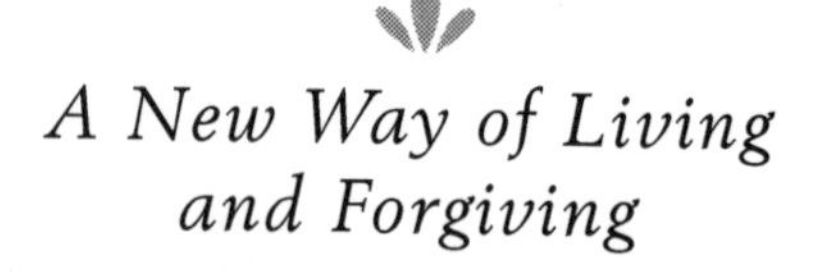

A New Way of Living and Forgiving

In the United States we imprison too many people. We have more than 2.2 million inmates in our prisons and jails. The impact on families is devastating.

In addition to imprisoning too many people, the sentences handed down are too long. We would benefit from studying European sentencing practices, which are far less harsh than ours. In the 19th century, de Tocqueville and Dickens traveled to America to study our prison practices. They were both deeply disappointed with what they found. When it comes to sentences and prisons, we should be the ones crossing the Atlantic to learn from Europe.

The needs of those sent to prison for the most part go unmet. Most prisoners are very poor. This has always been the case. In 1900, New York prisons doubtless were filled with people from Ireland, Italy and Eastern Europe — the poorest of the poor in the city at the time. Among today's poor, black and Hispanic men are in prison in huge numbers.

Prisoners are poorly educated. They have low, or zero, job skills. Many are addicted to drugs, alcohol or both. Some are mentally ill. They present a major challenge to society and to prison officials. And also an opportunity for transformation, being in prison seven days a week, 365 days a year.

And when prisoners are released to the community, they face a whole new set of barriers, making it difficult for them to obtain jobs, housing and access to public benefits. The collateral consequences of criminal convictions can be devastating to men and women returning from prison.

Late one Friday afternoon, as the sun is setting over the magnificent Hudson River, I travel by train to Sing Sing Correctional Facility to attend an inmate performance of "West Side Story", a project of Rehabilitation Through the Arts.

Some inmates have led lives similar to the roles they are performing; members, not of the Jets or Sharks, but of other gangs. Lives of violence, including murder. They share something else with the gang members in "West Side Story" — an aspiration to live a better life.

Inmates sang "Somewhere":

> There's a place for us,
> Somewhere a place for us.
> Peace and quiet and open air
> Wait for us
> Somewhere.
>
> Somewhere
> We'll find a new way of living,
> We'll find a way of forgiving
> Somewhere.

The eloquent words of Stephen Sondheim offer a beacon of light to those affected by our deeply flawed criminal justice system.

A new way of living in our country, where there will be less violence and destructive behavior.

A new way of living for the many millions of Americans in poverty. Poverty is poisonous and corrosive, destroying families and individuals, and leading to abandonment, addictions, mental illness and violence against family, neighbors and the community. Fighting poverty is the most effective way to fight crime.

A new way of forgiving, where prison is the last resort for lawbreakers and where prison sentences are fair.

A new way of forgiving, where prisons effectively address addictions and education and employment needs.

A new way of forgiving, where prisoners returning to society are treated, not as pariahs, but welcomed as prodigal sons and daughters. [2007]

APARTMENT/OFFICES

A Strong Sense of Place

How small to others, but how great to me! — Ovid

I have lived in the same 3½ room, sixth floor, rent controlled apartment at 155 East 73rd Street since 1964. When I began apartment-hunting two years after finishing law school, this was the first apartment I saw, located on a lovely street of carriage houses between Lexington and Third Avenues, in a 1929 building with high ceilings, a fireplace and a view of the dome of Saint Jean Baptiste, my favorite church in the city.

I immediately fell in love with the apartment. For a newly-minted lawyer earning $6,000 a year, to live on the fashionable Upper East Side without paying an exorbitant rent, in the wealthiest postal zone in the country, was the closest to heaven I was likely ever to achieve.

Other apartment hunters thronged the rooms. I caught fragments of their conversation. "Too small." "Our furniture will never fit." Here I was at a distinct advantage, owning only one chair. For me, small was good. (Thoreau: "I had three chairs in my house [on Walden Pond]: one for solitude, two for friendship, three for society.") In the first and last residential real estate transaction of my life, I turned to the building superintendent and said, "Yes!"

Now I am like a barnacle attached to a ship's hull. A few years ago, when the apartment was about to be painted — the walls were screaming, "paint us!" — the idea came to me to vacate the premises and stay at the Hotel Wales at 93rd Street and Madison Avenue. On arriving at the hotel, I became ill. Twenty blocks were too many for my system to absorb. I was homesick for the pavement and carriage houses on my block. A speedy recovery ensued upon my return.

I grew up three blocks from the Hotel Wales at 70 East 96th Street, inheriting my strong attachment to real estate from mother, who lived in her 16th floor apartment for decades. Joseph Brodsky, the Russian-born essayist and poet, writes of Russians and their attachments: "I am prepared to believe that it is more difficult for Russians to accept the severance of ties than for anyone else....For us, an apartment is for life, the town is for life, the country is for life. The notions of permanence are therefore stronger; the sense of loss as well." (Brodsky suffered many painful severances in his lifetime. Accused by Soviet authorities of being a "literary parasite," he served time in an Arctic Circle labor camp. At night in his bunk he read poetry. He was expelled from the Soviet Union in 1972 and came to live in the United States. He is buried in the Venice cemetery on the island of San Michelle, a city, like his native St. Petersburg, of islands, canals and palaces.)

This same strong sense of place extends to my workplace. Fourteen years of my life have been spent in an office at 54 Greene Street in SoHo, between Grand and Broome Streets, in a cast-iron building. From my desk on the second floor I look upon surrounding cast-iron buildings, the original 1870 glass in the large windows creating a distortion — an Impressionist painter's dream. (At the Metropolitan Museum of Art, I learn that the French painter Edouard Vuillard found inspiration simply by looking out his Paris apartment window. Between 1909 and 1928, he painted 60 views of the Place Vintmille.)

The view is not of barren rooftops, as with skyscraper offices I had previously occupied, but of sidewalks teeming with life. I like the old-fashioned tin ceiling. In the summer we place flower boxes on the wide window ledge. In this mixed-use building I see children and dogs in the elevator. Granite sidewalks. Bishop's crook lampposts. A small-town atmosphere. The creative juices of SoHo, with filmmakers across the street paying us $120 a night to keep our office lights on for film-making at night.

Passing a subway newsstand one day, my eye is drawn to a familiar scene: On the cover of "The New Yorker" is portrayed the façade of 54 Greene Street and the windows by my desk.

Alas, all this came to an abrupt end over the summer when the building owner told me that our lease would not be renewed. I was shattered. The stay at the Hotel Wales lasted three days; this would be forever.

And so began the tedious task of finding a new office. After viewing numerous unremarkable spaces, I came upon a building at 281 Park Avenue South at 22nd Street owned by the Federation of Protestant Welfare Agencies. According to a Landmarks Preservation Commission report, this 1894 building "takes its form from the great Medieval and Renaissance town halls and guild halls of Belgium and Holland."

We moved in September. A few days later, on the excuse of checking the mail box at the old office, I returned to 54

Greene Street. The office walls already had been knocked down for the new tenant. My battered wooden desk, used by me for 23 years but too large for the elevator in the new place, stood forlornly in the empty space, covered with plaster dust. Returning was a mistake.

Like a forest animal intent on making a new lair his own, within days of arriving at 281 Park Avenue South, and with the help of colleagues, I covered the walls of my new office with pictures of favorites of mine from history and literature. (Missing from the walls are my college and law school degrees and certificate of admission to practice law in New York State, thrown out by an overzealous housekeeper of mother, along with my college thesis on George Eliot.)

From my fifth floor office windows I have new views: Calvary Church, Park Avenue South, and in the distance, the trees of Union Square.

I spend my first few days prowling through the new neighborhood. Gramercy Park is around the corner. Nearby are the Flatiron Building, Madison Square Park and the courthouse of the Appellate Division, First Department — "This small marble palace...Corinthian columned," as described in the "AIA Guide to New York City" — where I was sworn-in as a lawyer in 1964. I go to the Greenmarket at Union Square to purchase fresh corn and Macoun apples. (I serve as a legal adviser to the Greenmarkets in the city.) I begin to feel there is a life after SoHo.

Had Columbus asked me to join him on his voyages of discovery, being rooted to my city — Seville, in this hypothetical — I would have declined. This crustacean has a too strong sense of place. I would have stayed in Seville to enjoy the oranges. [2010]

The Books Pile Up and So Do the Excuses

Returning home late at night, I unlock the apartment door and am shocked to find books scattered on the living room floor. Has the apartment been burglarized? Nothing so dramatic. A pile of books had toppled over from its own weight.

My apartment is awash with books, a testament to a penchant for both literature and clutter. With no cellar or attic — those safety nets for ownership excess — with not even a storage bin in the apartment house basement, books continue to pile up. The growing pile now conceals the Picasso reproduction of Don Quixote and Sancho Panza on the wall.

My books are in disarray, with no alphabetical or subject-matter coherence.

"Toss some books out," suggests a friend. Oh, how little you understand the acquisitive habits of a reader! The word "deaccession" is not part of our vocabulary.

Another friend advises, "Put your books in order." I contain myself from bursting out, "And why don't you straighten out the mess in your closets?" Tasks such as these — closet cleaning, book sorting — are much contemplated, but rarely performed.

Disorder seems a part of my life. On the floor by the fireplace, there always will be piles of books, along with a wooden lobster buoy I found along the Maine coast, an Indian copper pitcher and my bicycle.

And book piles will continue to rival the height of the mantel above the fireplace, where will be found a home run baseball from a Yankee game; a boomerang; a bottle containing sand from the Syrian desert; a bust of Richard Wagner; a photograph inscribed by Tolstoy to my grandfather; family pictures; pictures of my sister's cat; a cloth camel from Egypt; family pewter candlesticks; a flag from Public School 112 in Brooklyn where I served as principal for a day; my godson's creation, a clay gargoyle given to me twenty years ago; and the facsimile of a key made in 1812 for the door of New York's City Hall.

I don't fret about the disorder. Rather than spending too much time searching for a favorite book, I go out and buy another copy. I now own several copies of "David Copperfield" and "The Plague".

But I have one concern: Jenny, my sister's cat. She stays with me when her family is travelling. Jenny is a leaper, bounding from floor to windowsill to kitchen counter with ease. When Jenny is visiting, I dare open windows only from the top. Were she to leap on a pile of books, she would bring it down. I could never forgive myself if Jenny were crushed to death by the 29 volumes of the "Encyclopaedia Britannica" (11th edition, 1910).

[2006]

My Street

The arrival of spring encourages new undertakings. Having lived on 73rd Street between Lexington and Third Avenues for decades, I resolve to learn something about the buildings on my street and their history, buildings I have passed thousands of times, day and night, at all seasons of the year.

The first residential structures on the Upper East Side were row houses built in the early 1860s and sold to families of modest means. As the 19th century drew to a close, mansions built for the city's wealthiest residents on Fifth and Madison Avenues replaced many of the row houses west of Park Avenue. Wealthy New Yorkers did not consider the streets east of Park Avenue as desirable places to live, being too far from Central Park and the fashionable avenues. Along streets like mine, row houses were demolished to make way for carriage houses. The mansion owners wanted their private carriages and horses nearby, but not so close that the noise and smells of stables would mar the exclusive character of Fifth and Madison Avenues.

Two row houses remain on my street today. No. 171, built in 1860, with its unusual cast-iron veranda, and No. 175. The latter endures probably because the owner, Daniel Healey, in 1896 had the foresight to convert the building from a private residence to a blacksmith shop to serve the nearby carriage houses and commercial stable.

Each of the eleven carriage houses on my street is a two-or-three-story structure, with separate entrances for vehicles and pedestrians. The carriage houses are designed in a variety of styles: Romanesque Revival, Beaux-Arts and neo-Flemish Renaissance. When first built, the front room on the ground-floor level was used for carriages, and the rear room contained stalls for horses. On the upper floor might be found a hayloft and living quarters for the coachman and groom.

On a recent sun-filled Sunday afternoon, with winter in full retreat and spring each day gathering strength, I stood on the sidewalk examining the twin carriage houses Nos. 161 and 163 adjoining the apartment house where I live. Both buildings are ornamented with equestrian details I had not noticed before. The keystone over the vehicular entrance at No. 161 is in the form of knotted reins; at No. 163 the keystone takes the shape of a saddle pouch. Above each ground floor window can be seen horses heads carved in relief.

Only the very wealthy could afford to build and maintain private carriage houses. The roster of early owners of carriage houses on 73rd Street reads like a Who's Who of American wealth: Vanderbilt, Gould, Harkness, Marquand, Pulitzer. They could afford to hire architects of national prominence. Thus, Richard Morris Hunt in 1883 designed No. 166, the first carriage house built on 73rd Street, for Henry Gurdon Marquand, a real estate, banking and railroad tycoon. A decade later Hunt was commissioned by Marquand, who was then president of the Metropolitan Museum of Art, to design the museum's

Fifth Avenue façade. (Hunt's other commissions include the bronze doors of Trinity Church and the base of the Statue of Liberty.)

Another architect, William Schickel, whose firm did the Church of St. Ignatius Loyola on Park Avenue and 84th Street, designed the carriage house at No. 180 for Max Nathan, a manufacturer of railroad equipment. Both Nathan and Schickel were German immigrants. Much of Schickel's architectural work was for members of the German-American community. In New York City, then as now, ethnic ties help to forge business ties. The initials MN, for Max Nathan, carved into the façade above the vehicular entrance at No. 180, can still be seen.

Commercial stables met the needs of New Yorkers who did not own private carriage houses. At the S. Kayton & Co. Stable, built in 1890 at No. 182, neighborhood residents could stable their own horses, or hire a horse and carriage.

By the 1890s, a revolution in transportation was underway with the manufacturing of the first horseless carriages in the United States. In 1908 the stable became a garage. Two years earlier, directly across the street, a garage, designed by Charles F. Hoppe in the Beaux-Arts style with a crowning mansard roof, was built for the Automobile Realty Co. (Nos. 177-179). It is one of the earliest surviving garages in the city, and the only building on the street designed specifically for automobiles. Both garages continue in operation today.

With the automobile's arrival, the carriage houses on 73rd Street became private garages, and the coachmen became chauffeurs. Later, as the expense of maintaining a private garage became prohibitively expensive, most of the garages were transformed into residences.

Over the years, some of the carriage houses have been put to innovative use. John Woodruff Simpson, a founding member of the law firm of Simpson, Thacher & Bartlett, sold No. 161 to Edward S. Harkness, an heir of the Standard Oil fortune, who built a squash court and locker room on the second floor. In 1950 the building passed into the hands of the Dalcroze School of Music. For years I would be awakened on Saturday mornings by aspiring pianists pounding the keyboard. It is now a residence.

The Pulitzer family, which had purchased No. 166 from the Marquand estate, sold the building in 1924 to the MacDowell Club of New York. Named for Edward MacDowell (1860-1908), the noted American composer and concert pianist, the Club's purpose was to support the MacDowell Colony in Peterborough, N.H., where composers, writers and visual artists are provided with time and seclusion to further their creative efforts. Founding members of the club included the actress Sarah Bernhardt, the sculptors Daniel Chester French and Augustus Saint-Gaudens, and Charles McKim the architect. Later the building served as home for the Central Gospel Chapel of New York.

Having learned something of its history, walking on my street will never again be the same for me. Coachmen, grooms, blacksmiths, members of the nation's wealthiest families, architects, actresses and sculptors once passed daily along these sidewalks. Perhaps some rainy evening, when the lamppost light is reflected on the moistened street, I may see emerge from a carriage house a horse and carriage bound for Fifth Avenue, only to vanish before my eyes into the darkness of the night.

[1983]

Workday Views of Sky and Street

Before 54 Greene Street and 281 Park Avenue South, my VOLS office was on top of a food warehouse in downtown Manhattan. The first fourteen floors of our building on Varick Street are filled with pasta, prosciutto, salami, cheese, olive oil, smoked fish and pâté.

We are on the 15th floor. From my desk I see one river (the Hudson), two states (New York and New Jersey), three boroughs (Manhattan, Brooklyn and Queens) and many of the city's architectural landmarks (the World Financial Center, the World Trade Center, the Woolworth Building, the Municipal Building, and looking north, the Empire State, Chrysler and Citicorp buildings).

The views are so magnificent, both day and night, that I find myself getting to the office earlier in the morning and staying later in the evening. They energize me, and surprisingly, add to my concentration rather than detract from it.

Choosing an office involves basic lifestyle decisions. The nature of my job — working with law firms to provide civil legal services to poor people — suggests selecting an office in midtown around 42nd Street near many of the major law firms. But midtown happens to be the most congested and expensive part of New York City.

Instead, I chose TriBeCa, an area south of Canal Street near the Hudson River. By comparison, it is bucolic. Just how bucolic is evidenced by our closest neighbor, a stable for police horses. One day the sidewalk was blocked by a truck delivering hay from upstate New York. I like that. And I like the aroma of hay and horses.

The pace of life is leisurely; the setting is 19th century, with low red brick buildings and cobblestone streets.

The views of Manhattan's skyline won me over to the new space. I had told our real estate broker that sun and sky were essential. I spend a third, or more, of each day at the office. No one wants to look out on a shaftway!

A number of buildings I see from this office have, over the years, become an important part of my life. To the southeast is the Woolworth Building. Across the street from this building, by City Hall Park, each evening a hundred homeless people gather to receive a sandwich, soup, fruit and milk. Then they disperse to spend the night under the Brooklyn Bridge or in subway stations. In the midst of misery, the illuminated Woolworth Building stands as a beacon in the darkness; and so, perhaps, does the Coalition for the Homeless food program, carried out by volunteers seven nights a week, 365 days a year.

To the east I see the Criminal Courts Building on Centre Street. From time to time, I visit the court pens where recently arrested New Yorkers are confined while awaiting court arraignment. On this single New York City block the problems of urban America are painfully evident. The homeless sleep outside Housing Court. Family Court is a place of daily strife. Across the street, Department of Correction buses leave for the city jail on Rikers Island. Not quite what Katharine Lee Bates had in mind when she wrote the lines, "Thine alabaster cities gleam/ Undimmed by human tears!"

Also to the east, I see the old New York Life Insurance Company building, with its square clock tower designed by McKim, Mead & White. On March 5, 1842, on this block, at Broadway and Leonard Street, took place an important literary event in the nation's history. Ralph Waldo Emerson gave a lecture at the New York Society Library on the topic "The Poet." In the audience was a young man, age 23, named Walt Whitman who lived precariously as a newspaper reporter. Emerson asked whether "poetry is possible in the present time." He then went on to say, with more prescience than he realized, "The genius of poetry is here." To doubt that America's poet would yet appear "is to doubt of day and night."

Thirteen years later, Whitman sent to Emerson, to whom he was still a stranger, an unsolicited copy of "Leaves of Grass". Emerson read it and wrote to Whitman: "I find it the most extraordinary piece of wit & wisdom that America has yet contributed.... I greet you at the beginning of a great career... ."

The city I see from my office windows is a place of great contrast: beauty and human achievement, alongside suffering and despair.

[1991]

My Own Super

New Yorkers are not adept at fixing things; at least this one isn't.

We depend on building superintendents to rescue us. As a lifelong apartment-dweller, I call upon the super in my building to fix radiators that incessantly clank — "the hiccups of our central heating" — to quote Proust. To reignite the pilot lights on my stove. (I have an overly vigorous housekeeper who knocks them out at every cleaning.) To open and close stubborn windows. To install the living-room air conditioner in the spring and remove it in the fall. To attend to flooding from the apartment above. To help with DVD and cable television glitches.

Even more extensive services are provided in New York City office buildings. Maintenance staffs meet your every need, except for opening and closing windows, since in many buildings this no longer is possible.

But my small office in the heart of SoHo, where five of us work, is introducing me to new tasks because we are without a superintendent or maintenance staff.

Thus, in addition to performing the other duties required of an executive director, I climb a ladder to change light bulbs. This is no ordinary ladder, for the ceiling in our cast-iron building is 16 feet high. When I reach the top and am face to face with the original stamped-tin ceiling,

I try not to look down. I do not like heights. A colleague hands me the new bulb which I install.

I change the water-cooler bottle in the supply room, always a perilous juggling act to prevent spillage. It is less dangerous than in the old days when the bottles were glass.

On Tuesday afternoons after 4 p.m., I collect recyclable paper from the wastebaskets and place it in see-through plastic bags. I drag them through the hallway to the elevator and then to the street for pickup in the evening. It is a constant wonder to me how a small office can generate so much paper.

When I am the first to arrive in the morning, I unlock the elevator to gain access to our floor and turn on the lights and office equipment. During the day I make bank deposits — I only wish I had to make many more such trips to the bank — and at night take letters to the corner mailbox.

My new responsibilities are not without their mysteries. Why does the elevator not work on certain days? I believe it dislikes very cold weather. Why does the office doorbell ring when no one is there? I believe it is activated by passersby on the street who use cell phones.

Being on the second floor, I like to have the office relate to the street below. This means my hanging a Christmas wreath in one of the large windows during the holidays, and in the spring, placing flower boxes on the window ledge.

In the course of my activities, I converse with the window cleaner, contractors, computer expert, electrician, locksmith, telephone company representative, mail carrier and building owner.

Variety in life is appealing. I enjoy these tasks and encounters, a contrast to my usual life as a lawyer sitting at a desk with piles of papers.

But enough of writing. I must lay my pen aside. The radiators are clanking ominously and there is a steady dripping from upstairs. Action is needed now, not words!

[2000]

Ups and Downs

Horizontal travel is a daily part of New Yorkers' lives. We walk and bike on city sidewalks and streets. We take cabs and buses or speed under congested avenues on steel rails.

But vertical travel is not uncommon. Elevators play an important role in every New Yorker's life.

I grew up living on the 16th floor of an apartment house on the Upper East Side. On occasion, the door and elevator men in our building would go on strike. This was hard on mother and other older people in the building, but the superintendent was a kind man, and he would sneak mother up on the back elevator. During strikes, my dog and I walked 16 flights down and 16 flights up. Both of us found the whole thing a hoot.

My first job as a lawyer was on the 21st floor at 20 Exchange Place, just off Wall Street. The small law firm where I worked shared a bank of elevators with one of the biggest and wealthiest law firms in the city.

As I took these elevators every day with young lawyers from the other firm, I fantasized that the law firm's comptroller would mistakenly hand me a salary check, since the pay there was so much higher. It never happened.

Early on, I learned not to discuss sensitive matters — business or personal — while riding elevators. Everyone listens while pretending not to.

Once I was in an elevator in TriBeCa that got stuck. To pass the time, I read aloud to my fellow passengers the Department of Buildings Passenger Elevator Certificate in the elevator: "13 maximum no. of persons. 2,000 maximum no. of pounds."

We were less than 13. That was easy to determine, but what about our weight? I took out the pencil and notebook I always carry and questioned each passenger as to poundage. Some passengers were amused; others, not. But it did help time pass until our rescue.

I belong to the New York Society Library on East 79th Street. The library has a temperamental elevator. The gate snaps shut, threatening the noses and glasses of passengers. Comments from library members:

> "The elevators are terrifying."
>
> "The elevators are amusing."
>
> "About the elevators, how can you rate a museum piece?"
>
> "I love the elevator!"

At my office in SoHo, the elevator frequently breaks down. Since I'm on the second floor, the inconvenience for me is not great. But an upstairs neighbor is a child photographer, and she had a shoot on the day of a recent elevator breakdown.

On the sidewalk outside the building, rows of children's strollers were parked, watched over by the photographer's assistant. Parents, with child models in tow, climbed the steep wooden stairs to the fourth floor.

In my apartment house elevator on East 73rd, I encounter Calle. He is an Australian shepherd. He growls at me. I find this surprising, since my relations with dogs tend to be good. His owner said that Calle may have thought I was planning to steal one of his sheep. Calle has a sixth sense, for I do think a lot about lamb chops, my favorite meat dish.

Without elevators, how dull life would be. [2005]

Pictures on the Wall

At each of my offices, on a wall by my desk, I have placed six pictures: four prints, a photograph and a postcard. Each is framed. These are pictures of six of my heroes. (I have additional heroes and heroines, but the lack of available wall space and the expense of framing do not encourage expanding the group.)

Chekhov also enjoyed the company of his heroes. At one point in his life he left Moscow for Yalta, where he engaged a Tatar contractor to build a two-story house. In it, with its view of the steeply rising Crimea mountains, Chekhov placed a print of Pushkin and portraits of Tolstoy and Turgenev on the study wall by his desk. In the presence of these luminaries, no doubt inspired by them, he wrote "The Three Sisters" and "The Cherry Orchard".

At my office desk, less enduring prose is composed. Agreements, wills, pleadings, briefs — the stock and trade of a lawyer. Occasionally I raise my eyes from the legal papers to gaze at my heroes.

Four are familiar ones: Franklin, Jefferson, Washington and Lincoln. Not much originality in these selections. The other two are less known: King Henry IV of France (1553-1610) and William the Silent (1533-1584), leader of the United Provinces of the Netherlands.

Benjamin Franklin's zest for life I find irresistible. Though a New Englander by birth, his lifestyle was more cosmopolitan than Puritan. His worldliness shocked some American contemporaries but made him a great favorite at the French court. I am attracted by his optimism, love of life and deep patriotism.

Of my next hero, Thomas Jefferson, nothing more need be said of his talents than this felicitous comment of President John F. Kennedy to the Nobel laureates of the Western Hemisphere: "The most extraordinary collection of talent, of human knowledge, that has ever been gathered together at the White House, with the possible exception of when Thomas Jefferson dined alone."

George Washington resolutely led his countrymen to victory over the foremost military power of the day. Having himself overcome self-doubt and personal despair during the grueling War of Independence, no person had better claim than he to remind Americans that "It is not the part of a good citizen to despair of the Republic."

The photograph of Lincoln on my office wall was taken on August 26, 1858, less than a week after his first debate with Douglas. In the realm of fashion, Lincoln was a total flop. He appears in the photograph with a collar several sizes too large and tie askew. On the essentials he excels, his face conveying integrity, sensitivity and high intelligence.

Tolstoy said of Lincoln that he was a giant in both depth of feeling and moral power. To the proposal that he treat Confederate prisoners as Union prisoners were being treated at Andersonville, Lincoln responded: "Whatever others may say or do, I never can, and I never will, be accessory to such treatment of human beings." He granted generous pardons, rejecting the advice of those counseling revenge. On the issue of race, he said, "Let us discard all this quibbling about this man and the other man — this race and that race and the other race being inferior … and unite as one people throughout this land." Out of the ravages of war he sought a home for one national family.

Lincoln shared with King Henry IV and William the Silent an admirable trait: tolerance. Each was a man of tolerance living in intolerant times. In Paris, the St. Bartholomew's Day massacre of the Huguenots. In the Netherlands, six thousand people who would not abandon the Protestant faith being sent to the block, gallows, or pyre. Elsewhere Protestants burning Roman Catholics. In the 16th century, fanaticism was ecumenical.

How gloriously out of tune with his times were the words and deeds of Henry. The words: "There must be no more huge distinction between Catholics and Huguenots. All must be good Frenchmen, and let the Catholics convert the Huguenots by the example of a good life." The deeds: When laying siege to Catholic Paris, he had not the heart to maintain too harsh a blockade, lest his capital become a cemetery. He celebrated the taking of Paris with an amnesty, not executions.

My most recent acquisition, purchased last summer in the Netherlands, is a postcard portrait of William after a painting by Anthonis Mor. The Dutch national anthem, "Wilhelmus van Nassouwe," is named in his honor. The anthem has fifteen verses. In the first verse, William is described as "denvaderland Getrouwe" — "Devoted to the cause of the nation." No higher accolade can be bestowed on a person. Few people in history deserve it more.

As Philip II's grim policy of religious oppression unfolded in the Netherlands, William said, "I cannot approve of princes attempting to rule the conscience of their subjects." And, "To see a man burnt for doing as he thought right, harms the people, for this is a matter of conscience."

Tolerant deeds followed tolerant words. As Cicily V. Wedgwood notes in her brilliant biography "William the Silent", when Spanish negotiators hinted to William that his lands might be restored and his son be released from prison in Spain were he less stubborn on the issue of freedom of conscience, William would not budge an inch. In Ghent, he sought to persuade Calvinists to return churches seized from Catholics. When the Antwerp council proposed that a tax be levied exclusively against Catholics, William convinced them that it was wrong to penalize their fellow citizens in a war being fought for tolerance. His views upset Calvinist and Catholic alike, for William was at odds with his age.

Henry, William and Lincoln each had the personal misfortune to rule at a time of civil war. Civil wars generate furious hatred. Each suffered death by assassination.

My six heroes serve as a source of continuing inspiration.

[1983]

PERSONAL

Tuxedo

At age 16 I purchased my first tuxedo. It has hung on me, and in my closet, for 45 years.

The year is 1953. I am a sophomore in high school. The day of my first formal dance is approaching.

I walk into a men's clothing store, Howard's, on East 86th Street. A sharp-eyed salesman swoops down on me. "A tuxedo? I have the perfect one for you."

Off the rack he takes a double-breasted tuxedo with wide satin lapels. I protest, "No one wears these things anymore." He responds, "The single-breasted tux is a passing phase." On and on he goes.

He has recognized me for what I am: a city bumpkin. At this stage in my knowledge of life and the world, he could sell me the Brooklyn Bridge. Instead, the silver-tongued one sells me the last double-breasted tux in the store, and perhaps the last one sold in the nation.

And so I go to the dance, after purchasing the obligatory gardenia corsage for my date. We waltz and waltz, becoming thoroughly dizzy since I waltz in one direction only. At other times we fox-trot, whatever the music, since the fox-trot is the only other dance I know. Throughout the evening I stand out in my double-breasted tuxedo like a remnant from a bygone era.

The years pass. I think about buying a new tuxedo to reflect the times I live in, but why spend hundreds of dollars on an outfit worn only a few times a year?

Additional years pass. Then at black-tie events I experience unusual sightings.

First one, and then several men are seen wearing double-breasted tuxedos. The old style is returning. As the 20th century comes to a close, I no longer feel like a member of Tommy Dorsey's band.

Now, at formal events, I receive compliments on my tuxedo. "So elegant!" Miracle of miracles, the pants still fit. They are a little tight, but I can breathe, which is the important thing.

How prophetic you were, Mr. Salesman, wherever you are.

[1998]

Keys

When I'm walking on the streets of New York City, I hear a jangling sound. It is not change in my pocket but the 13 keys I carry. I feel like a jailer. The weight makes holes in my pockets.

I live a life of relative simplicity. No car. No country house. No safe-deposit box. Modest possessions. A small apartment. Why the need for so many keys?

Let me examine them one by one.

The key with the distinctive red plastic top unlocks the two doors leading from the street into my apartment house. The doors are open until 11 p.m. when the doorman leaves. When I arrive home late on a bitterly cold night, how reassuring it is to reach for the red key and enter the building. Warmth lies within.

A small key on my key ring opens the mailbox by the elevator.

On the sixth floor where I live, I have two locks on the apartment door. The cylinder on the top lock sometimes gets stuck. I jiggle the key to no avail. I have to ask the super for help. He is able to open the door with a duplicate key. The lock needs fixing.

I keep my bicycle in the living room, leaning against the fireplace screen. In the rough-and-tumble city I have chosen to live in, a heavy chain is necessary to secure a bicycle to lampposts on the street. Also a front-wheel lock. Two keys are for my bike.

My office in SoHo requires a whopping seven keys: one to open the door at the front entrance on Greene Street, another for the door leading to the mailbox, and a third for the mailbox. Then I need a key for the elevator to gain access to the second floor and a key for the office door.

The building also has a door on Broome Street, the original entrance to this 1870 cast-iron structure. It is much used, since the elevator often breaks down. The door leads to three steep flights of wooden stairs. The seventh key is for the fire door separating the stairs and the second-floor hallway.

When I walk up and down the wooden stairs, I am transported back in time to the 19th century and the world of Dostoevsky and St. Petersburg. Only the smell of cabbage soup is missing. [2000]

Shoelaces

A woman stopped me on the street to point out that a shoelace of mine had come undone. This often happens. Though the beneficiary of 19 years of the finest education this country can provide, I never learned the proper way to tie my shoelaces.

Perhaps I was absent from school the day it was taught. Or shoelace-tying may not have been part of the curriculum, and the failure to teach me lay at home. Or perhaps I was taught both at home and school, but was a poor student and the failure is mine.

In any event, following the woman's helpful comment — for you can trip on a shoelace trailing on the sidewalk — I leaned against the wall of a New York City apartment building and, standing on one leg, cranelike, tied the lace the only way I know how: two slipknots. Soon thereafter, the lace again came undone.

Other places where I tie laces in the course of the day are park benches, benches on subway platforms, and in the privacy of a telephone booth. (Between shoelace tyings, I found time to write this piece.)

When I am close to home, I don't bother tying the lace if it has become loose. Why expend the energy, since once I arrive at home, off come the shoes.

I do trip on my laces from time to time. Once a lace got caught in the chain of my bicycle. The result: a shredded shoelace.

I learn, courtesy of the Random House website, that the plastic or metal tip of a shoelace is called an aglet. It protects the feazings — the unraveled part at the end of a lace.

The composer Richard Wilson also has trouble with his shoelaces. He alerted me to a story about Gustav Mahler in a biography by Henry Louis de la Grange: "His shoelaces kept coming undone, and Alma (the future Mrs. Mahler) was touched by the childish awkwardness with which he invariable chose the highest and most uncomfortable places on which to rest his feet while he did them up again."

A Vasser student of Professor Wilson's has referred him to a website offering instruction on the tying of square knots.

I consulted the owner of the local shoe repair shop on Second Avenue. Once a dairy farmer in Wisconsin, at age 32 he started repairing shoes and has been doing so for a quarter century. He tells me he sells lots of laces, but does not offer to serve as my lace-tying instructor.

Given my interest in shoelaces, I spend time looking at people's footwear. The best place to do this is on the subway. My research reveals that very few people have any difficulty keeping their shoelaces tied. I am embarrassed to see children on the way to school, all with perfectly tied laces.

Why, you may ask, don't I seek out a five-year-old to teach me to tie my laces properly? My response: Dear Reader, at my age, it is not easy to abandon the practice of a lifetime. And then there is the matter of pride.

I could switch to loafers, thereby cutting this Gordian knot and avoiding the whole business of slipknots and square knots. But that would be too easy. Better that I now add to my list of resolutions for the New Year the goal of learning to tie my shoelaces. [2005]

Shoe Polish Box

Once a month, on a Sunday night, I polish my one pair of black dress shoes.I place a newspaper on the kitchen counter and go to a closet in the bedroom. On a shelf is a battered shoe polish box.

This wooden box is the only object I've ever made with my own hands. I made it in carpentry shop at elementary school. The teacher helped me. Using a pencil and ruler, with a firm hand he drew straight lines on a wooden board. I was to follow each line with a saw.

I did my best, but I was inexact. Each piece had a jagged end. I nailed the pieces together to form the box, but none were aligned. Two hinges were used to attach the cover. I painted the box blue, my favorite color.

I brought the box home and received polite parental praise for it. Both mother and the shop teacher must have realized that my future, whatever it might hold, lay not in the manual arts.

To this day, the box contains a tin of black shoe polish, a brush for applying the polish, a hand brush and a cloth for polishing and shining. I should polish my shoes more often. Walking as much as I do on New York City streets, they become scuffed. My reluctance comes from laziness and an inability to polish shoes without blackening my fingers.

Years after this introduction to carpentry, when I was serving as a counselor at a boys' camp in Maine, I was put in charge of the wood shop. My selection made no sense, but things worked out well.

I had a talented young assistant who taught the campers what they needed to know about carpentry. My responsibility lay in preventing the boys from hammering their fingers, or doing worse bodily harm with a saw. Much of the time in the shop I read Somerset Maugham's, "Of Human Bondage".

After polishing my shoes in the kitchen, I return the box to its shelf in the closet. My shoe box has served me well for more than 50 years; a functional, if not aesthetic success. It is one of my oldest possessions, and the only one remaining from my childhood. [2001]

Clothes

The arrival of spring seems a good time to examine my wardrobe. Let me start with my footwear and work up.

I wear low black sneakers most days. Very discreet. Most people consider them to be shoes. They are excellent for long walks on the hard concrete sidewalks of New York City. (In SoHo some sidewalks are granite from New England quarries.)

For formal occasions — a dinner party, the opera, funerals — I take from a closet shelf my elegant black English shoes. On the days I wear them, I hope it doesn't rain or snow.

My socks are made in Turkey. Three pairs for $5, purchased from a Chinese street vendor three blocks from where I live.

My pants are brown corduroy. They are sturdy, except for the pockets with holes from the weight of the keys I carry. As the holes grow larger, I lose more change.

I haven't owned a sports jacket for years, preferring to wear suit jackets from suits whose pants have worn out. I used to think huge moths inhabited my closet, for the jacket linings have large holes. But it's friction, the contents of my jacket pockets — keys, glasses (two pairs), pen, pencil, notebook and other assorted objects — rubbing against the material.

The ties I wear reflect personal attachments. A blue tie with the New York City seal in gold, bearing the date 1625 — the year the Dutch West India Company established New Amsterdam, and a crimson tie with the winged Lion of St. Mark in gold thread, symbol of Venice.

I wear the same tie day after day. In the rush of dressing in the morning, it is easier to reach for the familiar rather than spend time choosing from an assortment.

I save for last the pièce de résistance, my Borsalino. This felt hat is very expensive. I dare not have it cleaned. Decades ago, men all wore hats. No longer. Gone are most hat stores and with them, hat cleaners. Now when

I have a hat cleaned, it shrinks, while my head remains the same size.

I work for a nonprofit organization. When I visit a foundation seeking funds, I wear the sneaker/corduroy pants/suit jacket ensemble. This is my supplicant outfit. The last thing I want is to look prosperous.

For grand occasions, in addition to black shoes, I wear a double-breasted blue suit. This is my prosperous lawyer outfit. Here, the last thing I want is to look impecunious.

On all occasions, because of bone spurs in both heels, I wear orthotics. They are my most expensive article of clothing. [2005]

Baseball Cap

Since grade school, I have worn a cap or hat. This summer I purchased an elegant Borsalino straw hat. On less formal occasions, I wear a baseball cap.

My loss of the baseball cap presents me with a dilemma. For years I have worn a Boston Red Sox cap, even though I am a New Yorker to the marrow. The fact is, I take little interest in baseball and don't root for any team. I wear a Red Sox cap because of its beautiful "B." In my mind, "B" is for Bill, my first name.

I go to a sports store to select a new cap. I try on a Boston Red Sox, Yankee and vintage Brooklyn Dodgers cap. The last one also features a "B." Wearing a Dodgers cap might make more sense, since Brooklyn has been a part of New York City since 1898.

None of the caps fit. I have a large head and need a 7 $^{7}/_{8}$ size hat. The choice comes down to the Red Sox or Yankees, both one size too small. (The Dodgers cap is even smaller.) Whether it fits or not, I am determined to leave the store with a baseball cap.

I ponder, trying each cap several times. Favoring the Yankees are my close ties to the city. But the Yankees win a lot. I identify with losers, and in this department the Red Sox excel.

Also, if I wear a Yankee cap, no one will talk to me on the street. New Yorkers are expected to be Yankee fans. Wearing a Boston cap elicits a host of interesting observations from passersby. I relish these verbal exchanges. I also enjoy the role of contrarian.

And so I walk out of the store into a Herald Square crowd wearing a Boston Red Sox cap. I have made the right choice. The comments start coming, I remind one gentleman that Boston is still a part of the United States.

Wearing my new cap, I am on my way by bicycle to Lincoln Center for an evening performance by the Kirov Opera of Tchaikovsky's, "Eugene Onegin".

This year marks the 150th anniversary of Central Park. As part of the celebration, a baseball game is being played on grass under 1864 baseball rules. I stop to watch.

A "striker" (batter) hits the ball to the outfield. A "scout" (outfielder) runs for the ball. He fails to catch it on the fly, but does so after one bounce. The striker is out under the rules.

Ah, memories of school days as an outfielder. I would have done better as a scout, catching the ball after the first bounce.

I raise my Boston Red Sox cap in tribute to Central Park and to baseball and proceed on my way by bicycle to the opera house. [2003]

A Furry Visitor

Jenny, my sister's cat, is spending 13 days with me. She is small, black and white, with green eyes. I observe those eyes close up, for her favorite position is lying on my chest, front paws folded under her, looking into my face. On occasion she sneezes, but her black, prune-size nose is small, so the impact is minimal.

It is not easy to eat, sleep or read with a cat lying on your chest. I shoo Jenny away. Sulking, she goes into the bedroom. Soon after, I hear the crash of falling objects. She has jumped on the bureau, and with her right front paw is systematically knocking things onto the floor, including a clock.

A cat with a temper, but also an affectionate cat. Wagner's "Parsifal" runs from 6:30 p.m. to midnight. When I return home from the performance, Jenny has not been fed for 16 hours, yet she craves affection more than food.

She inspects every inch of my 3½ room apartment. She is drawn to dark, cluttered closets. I find her paw prints on the bathtub and sink.

At dawn, Jenny jumps onto my bed and walks over me, as if I were a rug, to take her position by the window.

Like a "sidewalk superintendent" on city streets, she closely observes construction work being done on a nearby brownstone. She also watches birds in trees.

Jenny and I play. She takes pleasure in simple games, like pushing a crumpled sheet of paper across the wooden floor with her nose and paws. A filbert I have placed on the floor is batted around like a hockey puck. She joyfully tangles herself in string from a laundry bundle. She dances on the bedspread to prevent me from removing it at night, or making the bed in the morning.

Time passes quickly. The day for Jenny's departure arrives. I return home in the evening to find this note:

Dear Uncle Bill, Thanks for your very kind hospitality. I had a great time with you and hate to leave! I will try to adjust to my parents again, but will miss you.

Jenny

[2003]

Being Tall Has Its Shortcomings

I go down six steep stone steps from the street to reach the laundry. At the entrance to this basement establishment there is a sign, "Watch your head!!!" (Yes, three exclamation points, suggesting numerous past encounters of customer heads with the door frame.)

Good advice for me because at 6 feet, 3 ½ inches, I hit my head often, especially on doorways, chandeliers, street signs, kitchen cupboards and low-hanging prosciutto hams in gourmet food stores.

My godson, Tom, is 6 feet, 10 ½ inches. He almost never hits his head. (Note these measurements to the half inch. We tall people are a vain lot.)

I theorize that midrange tall people like me hit their heads more often than extra-tall people like Tom, since the latter group are ever vigilant about obstacles.

I test the thesis on Tom. He confirmed it and responded by e-mail, "The more often one has to duck, the less likely one will fail to do so."

I extend my research to historical figures. Lincoln stood 6 feet, 4 inches. I don't recall reading that he ever bumped his head. Perhaps he did, but his biographers did not consider it worthy of mention, given all the other things happening in his life.

Peter the Great stood 6 feet, 7 inches. Surely, I reasoned, he bumped his head.

Not at all. On the marshland where he founded St. Petersburg, there was nothing to bump your head against. The city did not yet exist. The greater danger for Peter lay at his feet: sinking into the marsh.

Called the "czar carpenter" by contemporaries, this builder of St. Petersburg made certain his palaces had high doorways through which he could pass unscathed. Woe to the courtier with low doorways who invited Peter to his palace. He would learn that Peter was quick to anger. (On the subject of Peter's temper, read Nikolai Gogol's short story "The Overcoat," where on a St. Petersburg street a phantom — Peter himself — frightens a policeman by shaking his fist at him and demanding, "What do you want?" The policeman flees the scene.)

Personal experience with doorways and other objects, as well as my own research, lead to an inescapable conclusion: "Watch your head!!!" [2005]

Punctuality

At Collegiate School, the high school I attended in New York City, these words appear under the old clock: "Improve the Flying Moments."

I strive to do so.

Each day has moments that can be transformed from wasted time to time well-used. An example: the time spent waiting for people who are late.

"Punctuality is the courtesy of kings." This was a favorite saying of mother's, although it never made any sense to me since courtesy need not concern a king. He's the boss. In the spirit of these words, I put a lot of effort on being punctual. When I am late, I feel acute distress. Few people share the same concern.

In New York City, we have numerous excuses for being late. Subway delays, traffic jams, blackouts, water-main breaks, malfunctioning elevators. A snowfall, however slight, immobilizes the city for days. On occasion I use these excuses myself. But even when transportation systems run smoothly and no disaster is imminent, some people are always late.

Late arrivals to my office don't bother me. I continue working at my desk until they come. But for those who keep me waiting at their office, or in a restaurant, or on a street corner, I can fume or use the time in a productive way. I prefer the latter.

I dip into the reading material I carry with me for this purpose. At present it is a collection of poems by Pushkin, Russia's great poet. This year is the bicentennial of Pushkin's birth. Since my time for pleasure reading is limited, given a busy workday and other activities, what better pursuit to undertake while waiting in a lawyer's office for a meeting to start.

I read Pushkin's "Autumn," written in 1833. Here he writes of the joy of poetic inspiration:

> The pen calls for my hand, the page
> demands the pen;
> Poetry then pours forth in
> lines of every hue.
> Thus may a galleon stand,
> becalmed and sleeping, when
> Suddenly comes the call!
> At which the scrambling crew
> Swarms up and down to spread
> the swelling canvas wide.
> The giant sallies forth, cleaving the
> Surging tide…
> Where are we bound?

Nothing that may occur at the meeting will come close to being as stirring!

I am trying to extend these brief periods to other times of the day by reading on buses and subways, or when soaring to the top of office skyscrapers in elevators. Or reading at the gym when on an exercise bike.

At these times, to borrow from Boswell, my mind enjoys "ease and elbowroom." [1999]

A Landlubber Gets a Taste of the Sea

I report to Petersen's Boatyard, arriving with my possessions stowed in a sailor's bag — actually, a laundry bag — just as Ishmael would have done when boarding the Pequod in "Moby-Dick".

A sailing adventure awaits me. The voyage: Nyack, New York, to New London, Connecticut. Vessel, "The Venture", a performance sailboat of cutter design. Length, 40 feet; mast, 55 feet; beam, 11 feet. Crew: Captain S. Hazard Gillespie, approaching his 94th birthday; cook, the captain's "young brother," David; first mate, Richard; second mate, Matt, who, at 30, brings the average age of the crew down to 66; cabin boy, the writer of this piece.

My fellow crew members are experienced sailors. My experience is as a land-loving urban dweller. The movement of the earth only excepted, I prefer not being in motion, especially not being bounced around in a boat. I am on "The Venture" because of the advocacy skills of Captain Gillespie who charmed me into this undertaking.

I hope our journey fulfills the title chosen for a work by Felix Mendelssohn: "Calm Sea and Prosperous Voyage."

Our first stop is beneath the George Washington Bridge. Here we anchor for the night. The shimmering lights of this magnificent bridge are seen through the mist. Across the river, on the New York side, silver passenger trains speed north and south. Airplanes overhead prepare to land at city airports. Geese and cormorants fly above the water. From the ever restless city, sounds of drums and sirens.

At 6 a.m. we leave our anchorage and proceed down the Hudson River on an ebb tide. The river is choppy. Even at this early hour, many ferries and water taxis cross the Hudson, taking people to work. The wake of passing vessels causes our vessel to sway in ways I do not find comforting.

I try to focus on the buildings and streets we pass, places where I have lived, studied, worked and visited in a lifetime here. I see my city in ways not seen before.

We round the Battery and sail up the East River, going under the Brooklyn and Manhattan Bridges. From beneath the Manhattan Bridge, I see a Brooklyn-bound "N" train crossing the bridge, the same train I board at 60th Street and Fifth Avenue to travel to work. We pass East 73rd Street, where I live, and proceed under the Triborough and Hell Gate Bridges. At the Throgs Neck Bridge, we enter Long Island Sound. The Sound brings a world of lighthouses, buoy bells, lobster traps and oyster beds.

During the voyage, I perform my cabin boy duties as best I can, but I keep hitting my head on various objects. I am timorous about walking on deck for fear of falling into the Sound. When I take the wheel, the boat goes in the wrong direction. I come to realize the complexity of sailing, with its constant concerns about tides, weather, rocks, navigation and avoidance of other vessels.

I will never be a sailor. Why pretend? I choose to sit on a comfortable cushion by the wheel to admire the views, enjoy the sea breeze on a hot day, engage in conversation with captain and crew, and partake plentifully of the cook's fine meals.

The captain and I sleep on deck by the wheel. On the third night at 1 a.m. it begins to rain. We crawl out of our sleeping bags and make ineffectual attempts to put up rain-protecting canvas. (Do I hear gulls laughing at our efforts, or is this part of a dream?) I finally succeed in snapping the canvas in place and return to my sleeping bag, feeling a measure of satisfaction in having completed one nautical task.

The next morning, Captain Gillespie, with gratitude for my services the prior night, elevates me from cabin boy to seaman.

I now feel worthy to extend to you, Dear Reader, this greeting of George Eldridge, who 130 years ago established an essential mariner guide, "The Eldridge Tide and Pilot Book": "Yours for a fair tide." [2004]

Watching the World Come In

In my early teens, I read the shipping news in "The New York Times" to learn the departure times of trans-atlantic liners.

The Queen Mary, with her three smokestacks, was my favorite. When her sailing time was announced, I would ride my bicycle from East 96th Street, where we lived, to the North River passenger-ship piers on the West Side. (The Hudson flowing past Manhattan is known also as the North River.) Here I watched passengers arrive by taxi to board the ship. The idea of a journey by sea of thousands of miles starting at West 55th Street — from the New World to the Old — fascinated me.

Following the Queen Mary's departure, I would bicycle four miles to the Battery at the southern tip of Manhattan. From this vantage point, I would see the Queen Mary emerge from the North River into New York Harbor and continue her royal progress toward the Narrows and the sea beyond. Not until the top of her last smokestack disappeared from view did I move from the spot.

Today, few transatlantic liners depart from New York. The shipping news has disappeared from the papers, but I still bicycle.

This past Fourth of July, I spent most of the day cycling the streets of Manhattan. I returned to the Battery. No ocean liner was in sight, but there was much to cheer about. The Independence Day celebrants in Battery Park highlight the diversity of the city's population, coming as we do from some 180 lands. In a plaza by the river, these lines of Walt Whitman are embossed on an iron fence:

> City of the world! (for all races
> are here,
> All the lands of the earth make
> contributions here;)
> City of the sea!

Whitman would bemoan the dearth of ocean-crossing passenger ships in the harbor, but applaud the diversity of the peoples making up his "City of the world!"

[1997]

Hear Ye!!! 'King' William Bares His Soul

A dream: If I were king....

Everyone would learn to speak a foreign language. This would include the king.

"Distinguished Disobedience" was acknowledged by the Empress Maria Theresa of Austria with a special award. The tradition needs reviving. The award would be conferred on public officials who, ignoring rules and regulations, allow fairness and common sense to prevail.

The national toast would be one used during the Revolution: Perpetual itching and no scratching to America's enemies!

Once each year at Paris's Théâtre Français, at the end of the performance, the curtain rises to reveal a bust of Molière. All the actors then march on the stage with wreaths to crown the bust. During my reign major artists, living and dead, will be so honored.

Portraits of General Alfredo Stroessner, dictator of Paraguay, used to be everywhere, including in the living rooms of his opponents. I would move in the other direction, eliminating official portraits from post offices and replacing them with Monet landscapes. No bridge would be named for any public official not dead for at least fifty years.

Tolstoy, Chekhov and Ibsen would receive Nobel Prizes for literature. They were never so honored during their lifetimes. (Ibsen did enjoy one small piece of revenge when the Norwegian poet Bjornstjerne Bjornson received the Nobel Prize in Stockholm in 1903. Michael Meyer writes in "Ibsen, A Biography", that Bjornson tried to enter the palace through a side door but found his way blocked by a sentry. "My good man," Bjornson informed him, "I am Norway's greatest writer." "Oh," said the sentry, making way, "I beg your pardon, Herr Ibsen.")

I would follow the advice of Louis IX of France (Saint Louis): "do your utmost to avoid the sins that arise from war. Take care that you have been well advised before you act in any warlike manner, that your case is thoroughly reasonable...."

Better yet, the spirit of Pablo Casals would prevail. Asked what he would say if he could talk to all the people in the world, Casals responded: "I would say, do you like war? I am sure that all those millions of people would say 'No.' And then I would play a Bach piece for them."

How would posterity view my reign? On this I am one with the British conductor Sir Adrian Boult: "I don't care tuppence what posterity says about me! Have that! How's that for you?"

[1975]

New York and Venice

New York and Venice, both island cities. New Yorkers may not think ourselves an island people, but only the Bronx and a small portion of northern Manhattan form part of the North American mainland. The rest of us live on islands. For me, the most dramatic and beautiful feature of our skyline is not tall buildings but the magnificent bridges linking island to island, and islands to mainland.

Venice is a city of hundreds of islands linked by bridges. It is small and fragile, covering only 1,800 acres, with a resident population of about 65,000. New York is large and robust, with a population of 8.2 million. According to the city's official Green Book, the city covers an area of 305 square miles. Laid end to end, our city streets would extend 6,375 miles.

Venice provides me with the relaxing pleasures of a shipboard cruise without the unpleasantness of rolling seas and physical confinement.

In Venice, residents of all ages are keenly aware of the tides. This is not surprising, given the city's unusual setting:

> There is a glorious City in the Sea.
>
> The Sea is in the broad, the narrow streets,
>
> Ebbing and flowing; and the salt sea-weed
>
> Clings to the marble of her palaces.
>
> — Samuel Rogers

Sirens wail to warn Venetians of impending high water, *acqua alta*, from the Adriatic. Life in the city comes to a halt, like New York during a snowstorm. In low-lying areas such as the Piazza San Marco, raised wooden walkways are put in place. Every Venetian owns a pair of high rubber boots.

New York is a city of many churches, but on my walks in the city I hear few church bells. In a letter from Venice to his sister, Chekhov wrote, "There is a booming in the air because of the pealing of church bells."

The bells converse with one another. At 6:30 p.m., vesper bells of the church of the Gesuati begin the exchange. Across the canal on the island of Giudecca, the bells of Sant' Eufemia respond, followed by the neighboring bells of the Redentore. Their ringing awaken from slumber the bells of Santa Maria della Salute on the Grand Canal. From a bridge I see the tolling bells of the Redentore in their minaret-like towers. Minutes pass. Then one by one the bells disengage from the conversation, those of the Salute having the last word.

On a stone stairway on the Grand Canal, I watch the Venice version of midtown noon traffic on Fifth Avenue. Barges delivering fruit and vegetables; vaporetti, the waterbuses of Venice; boats of the carabinieri; gondolas; water taxis; a fire department boat — Vigil del Fuoco — with red flashing lights; a vessel of the Guardia di Finanza (tax collectors); garbage barges; a siren-blaring ambulance;New York and Venice are quintessential walking cities. From the Doghana (Customs House), I gaze upon the most splendid view of Venice, day or night: Palladio's church of San Giorgio Maggiore; the church of Santa Maria della Pietà, where Vivaldi served as choirmaster and resident composer; the Doge's Palace; the Marciana Library; and the domes of San Marco and its campanile, crowned by a golden angel. (Proust: "When at ten o'clock in the morning my shutters were thrown open, I saw ablaze in the sunlight...the Golden Angel on the Campanile of San Marco. In its dazzling glitter... it promised me with its outstretched arms...a joy more certain than any that it could ever in the past have been bidden to announce to men of good will.")

Walking at night in Venice, I go through deserted squares and narrow passageways. The overwrought imagination of this New Yorker makes these places seem sinister. They are not. When I am about to overtake Venetians, they do not nervously peer over their shoulders as we New Yorkers do, even on our well-lit, wide sidewalks. My closest encounter with crime in Venice: A handwritten sign at the San Marco vaporetto stop reading, "Caution Pik Pocket Near at You."

At night, from a vaporetto on the Giudecca Canal, I see the three windows of the room where I stay at the Pensione Seguso, illuminated by the lamp by my bed, making me feel very much a part of Venice.

Night sounds from my room: Water lapping against the stone embankment; voices of passersby; heels on stone walkways; cats fighting; the roll of thunder. I awaken to the sound of throbbing engines of arriving cruise ships and the singing of birds, perhaps even the chaffinch perched on the crossbar of the arcade in Giovanni Battista Tiepolo's painting in the nearby church of the Gesuati.

Through a lifetime of living in the city, I have come to know New York. Through my many visits, I have come to know Venice. Both cities are forever a part of me.

[2008]

A Letter Gets the Lights Turned Back On

As a frequent visitor to Venice over the years, I have acquired specialized knowledge of the city. Many visitors know the paintings of Giovanni Bellini, Vittore Carpaccio, Titian, Paolo Veronese, Giovanni Battista Cima da Conegliano and Jacopo Tintoretto. But I also have come to learn the names of the tugboats proudly guiding arriving and departing Mediterranean cruise ships along the Giudecca Canal. My favorites are Hippos, Maximus, Strenuus, Squalus, and Emilio Panfido.

From Room 10 at the Pensione Seguso overlooking the choppy waters of the Giudecca Canal — about as wide as New York's East River — I spend hours watching the procession of tugboats, water buses (*vaporetti* and *motoscafi*), and gliding over the water, ferries transporting cars and their drivers between the mainland and Lido.

I learned at a "Turner and Venice" exhibition that Turner annotated the backs of several watercolor studies with notes conveying the excitement he felt in being the temporary possessor of the Venice views he had from his hotel room. I feel the same as I gaze from the windows of my room.

About 6:45 each morning, tugboats head out to the lagoon entrance to meet arriving cruise ships. Among many boat sounds on the canal, I recognize the sound of tugs. Tugs are deep-throated, as befits their size, strength, status and responsibility. They are my Venetian alarm clock, reinforced by ringing church bells.

Soon the tugs return, guiding cruise ships by my windows to the Stazione Maritima.

A few years ago, my role in Venice changed from that of mere tourist to civic participant. Upon arriving, I was dismayed to find that Palladio's wonderful church, the Redentore (Redeemer), which I see from my windows, no longer was illuminated at night.

A joy of Venice in the evening is to walk on the Zattere, the promenade running along the Giudecca Canal from the maritime station to the custom house (Dogana di Mare). From the Zattere I would gaze across the dark waters of the canal at the illuminated Redentore on the island of Giudecca. Now this joy had been snatched away from me, and far worse, from every Venetian.

On returning to New York, I set to work on a letter comparing the misdeed to extinguishing the illumination of the Empire State Building, Brooklyn Bridge or Statue of Liberty. We New Yorkers would never tolerate this, nor should Venetians with regard to the Redentore. Landmarks such as these deserve to be seen every hour of the day and night.

After asking a friend to translate the letter into Italian for me, I mailed it to "Il Gazzettino", the leading Venice newspaper.

The editor did not toss my letter into the wastebasket. Nor was it put in the "Letters to the Editor" section. No, the editor placed it in the center of the front page, supplemented by interviews with church and city officials. None of their justifications for turning off the lights made any sense.

The Redentore is again illuminated. I claim full credit. If I lived in Venice, this might have launched a brilliant career in politics for me, although first I would need to learn Italian in the Venetian dialect.

Coming from faraway New York, I derive full satisfaction each time I am in Venice by gazing from the Zattere on the illuminated façade and dome of Palladio's magnificent church, and then once again looking at it from Room 10 of my pensione before falling asleep. [2005]

Practical and Poetic

A biography describes Anton Chekhov as being both practical and poetic. To me, this seems a desirable balance in life.

Being practical is a necessity. The monthly rent must be paid, along with gas and electric bills. (I recall blackouts at home when I was growing up. Mother, with all her other responsibilities, had forgotten to pay the electric bill. On those occasions, we dined by candlelight.)

Our lives need a degree of organization. Like living within our means. Completing tasks. Punctuality.

But there is more to life than paying bills and being organized. A poetic element is desirable. It can take different forms. Enjoying literature, music, art. Writing. Daydreaming. Being open to nature. "Look, look old mole! There, straight up before you, is the magnificent sun. If only for the instant, you see it." (Emerson)

Each day I combine the practical and the poetic.

Setting the alarm clock and rising when it rings is the essence of practicality. Listening to the birds sing outside my window while lying in bed is poetic.

Dressing for work and walking to the subway is practical. Selecting a route to the subway through Central Park is poetic, as is sitting on a park bench to write and enjoy the blossoming trees.

At the conclusion of my day, the mix continues. In the evening I read legal documents for meetings the next day, but the poetic slips in. I listen to an opera as I review the documents, and then — in the last waking hour of my day — read from a play, novel or biography.

The poetic has gained the upper hand, that is, until the alarm clock goes off seven hours later and a new day begins.

A life without being practical can be chaos. A life without poetry is half a life. Combine the two, and you have a satisfying life.

"If your everyday life seems poor, don't blame it; blame yourself; admit to yourself that you are not enough of a poet to call forth its riches...." (Rilke)

[2001]

BASKETBALL/OPERA

The Highest Court

My fondest dream as a lawyer: To appear on the highest court in the land. I refer to the basketball court located directly above the United States Supreme Court chamber.

From an article by Thomas Burr in "The Salt Lake Tribune" I learn of this sign outside the Supreme Court gym:

Playing Basketball and Weight Lifting
Are Prohibited While Court Is In Session.

Do Not Assume That Court Is Over!

Contact the Marshal's Office @ Ext. 3333
Before Starting These Activities On Court Days.

Mr. Burr writes: "A player dribbling the ball up there translates into big booms downstairs."

Hundreds of New York City lawyers share the same dream. They come from more than 50 law firms and play on Lawyers Basketball League teams in divisions with names such as Barristers, Counsellors and Defenders.

Law is a highly competitive profession. Here I set forth my credentials to play at the United States Supreme Court. Highlights from my basketball curriculum vitae.

My talents were recognized at an early age. Humphrey Fry, who taught English, history and mathematics at St. Bernard's School — my favorite teacher in 19 years of schooling — wrote of me in the 8th grade: "D is for Dean who is as thin as a lathe/His basketball excels his performance in math."

At Collegiate School I was the captain of the high school team. Basketball was then the center of my life. When walking my dog, I practiced dribbling on the street. To improve my rebounding skills, before going to bed, to the intense annoyance of the downstairs neighbors, I jumped up to touch a ceiling beam one hundred times.

Our high school record was spotty. We won home games, the result of low supporting beams in the gym. Visiting players had difficulty shooting over the beams. In away games, on an open court, we did less well.

That is, except against Staten Island Academy. We always beat them. Two days after each Staten Island game, I would bicycle from 96th Street to the ferry terminal at the Battery to purchase a copy of the "Staten Island Advance". With not much happening on Staten Island, our games were extensively covered. Being the top scorer, my name figured prominently in the articles.

In 1955, my senior year in high school, the "New York Post" named me to the private school all-city team as substitute center. Lou Rossini, the basketball coach at Columbia College, invited me up for an interview.

At Harvard I had every intention to try out for the varsity team, but was prevented from doing so by receiving two "D" grades — in economics and Spanish — making me ineligible for a varsity team and eligible for academic probation. The setback led me to drop basketball and change to intramural soccer and squash, and on warm spring afternoons, sculling on the Charles River. I emerged from college an honor student, but without the laurels that accompany successful athleticism.

I did not return to basketball until age 55. One day at the Lenox Hill Neighborhood House on East 70th Street, I was in the fitness room, bored to death using exercise machines, when a basketball player from the gym came up to me to say, "We need you." They had nine players. I would make the tenth. Since then, following my decades-long lay off, I have been playing several times a week to make up for lost time.

The group I play with ranges in age from 18 to 75. On the occasion of my next birthday, the age range will be 18 to 76.

Basketball is a generous sport to old-timers. On a soccer field I would last two minutes with the nonstop running. Basketball is a start and stop game — each stop an opportunity for me to catch my breath.

Also, while speed and reflexes diminish markedly over the years, my eye has not changed. I have a remarkably good shooting eye and win most shooting contests against far better players. Left unguarded, I score.

When a player in his twenties is assigned to guard me, I fall back on cunning. Before the game starts I ask him, "Do you have a grandfather?" He nods. "I want you to treat me as you would your grandfather." Politeness requires him to let me grab a rebound or two and grant me the space I need to launch a one-hander.

To prepare for my Supreme Court appearance, I have been addressing two negative aspects of my game.

First, I foul, not the result of an innate viciousness, but to slow down far younger and faster opponents.

Second, I swear. At a recent college game I came upon a "Sportsmanship Code of Conduct" posted on the gym wall. This provision shamed me: "Profanity will not be tolerated...[and constitutes] ground for removal from the Athletic Facility."

Yes, I am an offender, but in my defense, there are certain Old and Middle English words that cry out to be used when making an errant pass or missing a game-winning, unopposed layup. The words, I might add, appear in "The Oxford English Dictionary" (Sixth Edition), and doubtless in the five earlier editions.

As an attorney and counsellor at law and basketball player, I pledge to improve my behavior on both fronts to do honor to the court, the profession and the memory of Dr. James Naismith, inventor of the game.

My bags are packed. I am ready to play. I await to be summoned by the highest court in the land.

[2010]

Postscript:

The highest court has at last summoned me.

On a warm winter day in Washington, D.C., the sun brightly shines on the Corinthian columns of the United States Supreme Court. My instructions are to be standing by the John Marshall statue on the ground floor at 3 p.m. There I am met by Eric Nguyen, a law clerk to Justice Anthony Kennedy.

Eric leads me up four flights of stairs to the Supreme Court gymnasium. By taking the stairs, is Eric testing my physical endurance? Trying to wear me out before we play? Probably not, but we basketball players are a competitive and suspicious lot.

The gym is impressive, the only drawback being the low ceiling. I will need to adjust my high-arching one-hand shot.

I feel confident. My shooting has improved, the result of three one-hour training sessions from a professional basketball player, a gift presented to me by the board of directors on the occasion of my retirement from Volunteers of Legal Service. The board citation read: "This gift is not accompanied by a warranty that anyone can improve Bill Dean's basketball skills."

Eric turns out to have a good shot. We play a variety of shooting games. I suggest "Round the World." I excel at this game involving long one-hand shots and have chosen it because Eric won the foul-shooting contest. I need to establish my dominance.

Then we play one-on-one, not just shooting, but also running and dribbling. Eric wins the first game by a whisker in overtime. I win the second. Eric is respectful of my years — a half century separates us — giving me time and space to shoot. (This followed my inquiries concerning his grandfather.) I am appreciative. Now is a good time to stop, with both of us winners.

Following basketball, Eric takes me down to the second floor where he introduces me to several law clerk colleagues. The law clerks serve for one year. Each justice has four. He shows me his desk by a high window with a splendid view of the Capitol dome. We then visit the courtroom.

I thank Eric for his gracious hospitality, bid farewell to Chief Justice John Marshall in the lobby, and depart.

Over the years I have played basketball in many places. High in the Andes with Indian children where the air is so thin that the ball, when shot, flew over the backboard. At sea level in Amsterdam outside the Rijksmuseum, with its wonderful Rembrandts.

None can match this venue.

[2012]

A Day of Basketball and Opera

One Saturday morning I appear at my gym to play basketball for two hours. As noon approaches, I announce my departure. "How come?" teammates ask, since I am usually the last to leave. "Die Walküre", I respond, and depart without further explanation.

For the next five hours, I sit by the radio at home listening to the Metropolitan Opera broadcast of Wagner's magnificent opera.

What would Wagner's view on playing basketball before a performance be? We shall never know, since the game, invented by James Naismith in 1891, came after Wagner.

Basketball and opera have this in common: Both are physically demanding. Basketball involves running, shooting and rebounding. For members of the audience, Wagner makes demands on another part of the anatomy: "Sitzfleisch", to use the German word.

With the exception of "Die Meistersinger", which is inhabited by real people, Wagner's music has, for me, an extraterrestrial quality. The operas are long — Cosima Wagner wrote of her husband in her diary, "R. does not care for brevity" — but glorious.

Sometimes I watch basketball on television with the sound off while listening to an opera. This makes for interesting comparisons: Tim Duncan of the San Antonio Spurs leaping for a rebound; Tosca leaping from the ramparts of the Castel Sant'Angelo.

I have played basketball and attended operas for decades. I marvel at the talents and energy of players and singers. I know the rosters of both the Metropolitan Opera and the New York Knicks. It would be wonderful to have a Valkyrie or two on my basketball team. We would never lose. [2005]

Notes on the Ring

Day One, Monday. I arrive at the Metropolitan Opera for "Das Rheingold", prologue to Richard Wagner's "Der Ring des Nibelungen". This is the shortest of the four operas that make up "The Ring". Running time: an intermissionless 2 hours, 35 minutes.

My seat is in the last row of the Family Circle. The Family Circle is higher than the Balcony. Mountain goats would be challenged to reach my seat. Acoustically, it is the best seat in the house. Visually, the stage seems blocks away.

The opera begins. For a tall person like me, the leg-room is woeful. During the performance I twist and turn in my seat, assuming the shape of a pretzel.

Heat rises. It is very warm. I dare not whisper a word of complaint to my neighbor. Wagnerians are not forgiving of distractions.

Day Two, Tuesday. "Die Walküre". Running time: 5 hours, 15 minutes. I am wearing lighter clothing to avoid the heat problem and carrying roasted almonds and dried peaches to avoid the hunger problem.

I travel from my office to the opera house by the subway. The D train crawls up the West Side. Signal problems. The subway cars are jammed with people. Babies crying. Will I be on time? The Met is adamant about not seating latecomers.

On the subway I munch a sandwich. Wagner intended that his listeners arrive at the opera house in a relaxed and tranquil frame of mind, having reflected on the opera to be performed that day. This is not my situation.

Snacks notwithstanding, my mind wanders to thoughts of food during "Die Walküre". At the opera's conclusion, I am as hungry as a wolfhound. I partake of a cheeseburger and vanilla milkshake at an all-night diner.

Day Three, Wednesday. Rest day. No opera tonight. I relax by playing basketball at the gym and then watching a televised NBA playoff game.

Day Four, Thursday. "Siegfried". Running time: 5 hours, 30 minutes. When I stand by my seat, I can almost touch the gold ceiling of the opera house. I am becoming friendly with my seat-mates and the standees behind me.

Today, I left the office at 4:45 p.m. "The Ring" is all-absorbing. I am falling behind in my work.

Following the conclusion of "Siegfried", the 65th Street crosstown bus returning to the East Side through Central Park is jammed with Wagnerians who express strong views on the performance. Seldom do such spirited exchanges take place on a bus.

Day Five, Friday. Rest. Play basketball.

Day Six, Saturday. "Die Götterdämmerung". Six hours. This is close to the time it takes to fly from New York to London. Biggest "Sitzfleisch" challenge yet.

At the conclusion, thunderous applause, a standing ovation, bravos. Everyone in the house, all 3,800 of us, have shared an extraordinary journey. The standees, who have been upright for 19 hours, thump the wall paneling in approval.

I bid the occupants of row K farewell. I am one of the last people to depart from the hall. Rumblings are heard backstage behind the curtain as the remains of Valhalla are removed by the stage crew.

Past midnight, I walk from the opera house across Lincoln Center Plaza to my bicycle and ride home through Central Park. I need the cool night breeze on my face to revive me after the heat of the auditorium, and I want to reflect on the wonderful music I have heard. I feel very proud, and privileged, to have participated in this towering achievement of Western music.

I exit from the park at 72nd Street and Fifth Avenue. Several families stand on the sidewalk by my apartment house. They hold lit candles. It is Easter Sunday according to the calendar of the Orthodox Church. We are fellow celebrants. [2000]

On Stage, Just a Supernumerary, But...

The night of my Metropolitan Opera debut had arrived. As I approached the opera house, the colors of the Chagall paintings never seemed more bright, the crystal lobby chandeliers more sparkling, the red carpeted grand stairway more stately. I examined the poster for the evening's performance: Verdi's "Don Carlo", James Levine conducting, with Mirella Freni, Plácido Domingo, Louis Quilico, Nicolai Ghiaurov and Grace Bumbry. The Met had failed to list me as a cast member.

The dictionary definition of a supernumerary is "a person not a regular actor, but employed to appear as in a mob scene or a spectacle." I am to appear in the *auto-da-fé* scene in "Don Carlo" where religious and secular authorities, along with the faithful, assemble in Madrid to witness the burning of heretics condemned by the Inquisition.

Originally I had been scheduled to make my Met debut as a super in "La Bohème", but when the assistant stage manager, William McCourt, learned I was over six feet tall, he steered me to "Don Carlo". The "Don Carlo" director, John Dexter, wanted tall supers as bishops. Mr. McCourt assured me that *auto-da-fé* in 16th-century

Madrid would be more interesting than 19th century life among Parisian bohemians.

Supers are a varied lot. Some are opera buffs like myself. Some aspire to be singers, dancers or actors. Others aspire merely to be employed. Among the supers with me were a horticulturist, two organ builders, a cartoonist, a retired journalist, an undertaker, a teacher of Italian, an investment adviser and secretaries who work in law and advertising firms. Many have performed as supers for years. One of my colleagues appeared at the old Metropolitan Opera House in the 1926 American world premiere of Puccini's "Turandot".

Supers need not be singers. Indeed, we are forbidden to sing. We are to be seen, not heard.

At the first rehearsal for this new production, the 146 male supers in "Don Carlo", depending on size, age and shape, were transformed into bishops, monks, soldiers, Spanish lords and heretics. The seven women supers became ladies-in-waiting.

The chorus and some of the principal singers were already on stage as the supers marched on to the accompaniment of a piano. Confusion reigned. "We are missing monks like crazy," moaned a distraught Met official. I was placed at the front of the religious procession, with a fellow bishop at each side. At center stage the bishops were directed to make a right turn by the pit where the heretics awaited their fate. From my position on stage I gazed into the empty house. In the distance, barely visible to the naked eye, I made out the Family Circle, where I sit as a member of the audience.

When the burning of heretics was to commence, we did an about-face and proceeded upstage, avoiding collision with a column of soldiers moving downstage, and perched on a flight of steps, gazing malevolently at the heretics. King Phillip II (Nicolai Ghiaurov) and his Queen, Elizabeth of Valois (Mirella Freni) passed by. Soldiers arrived with torches to light the pyre.

At the conclusion of the first rehearsal, I walked past the dressing rooms for the principal singers and up a flight of stairs to our less elegant quarters. Costumes from different operas hung from pipe racks in the super dressing room. Wooden benches lined the wall.

My costume was in three parts: A gown of pongee reaching down to my ankles; a bishop's cope, similar to a long cape, of black quilted taffeta embellished with gold braid and encrusted with jewels; and as a headpiece, a black miter with gold braid and tails at the back, topped with a Maltese cross. When I walked, the cope trailed behind me. A fitter asked that I not dust the corridors with my costume.

On my way to the stage at the dress rehearsal, I passed a monk in a telephone booth and met the four Irish wolfhounds who appear in the first scene of the opera in the forest of Fontainebleau. Their names: Bryan, Dulcinea, Fionula and Nevin. (The Met backstage area is so vast I never did encounter the horse that appears.)

As we bishops neared the stage, we were told by an official in the wings to wait, followed by his cool, "Warning your eminences," and then a frantic, "Go! Go!" A group of monks coming off stage blocked our advance. Not until the ecclesiastic traffic jam could be unsnarled were the bishops able to proceed on stage to the now familiar spot by the heretics. While the singing continued, the assistant stage director, David Sell, walked about the stage giving instructions. He came over to me and pushed the miter further down on my head. It was so tight that I feared the circulation of blood might be cut off. But the cope was causing me greater concern, for as the bishops marched upstage, followed by the King and Queen, I tripped over it, and the cope started sliding to the floor. In the presence of James Levine, the company on stage, the orchestra, and an invited audience of Metropolitan Opera Guild members, a dazzlingly arrayed and bejeweled bishop was being transformed into a forlorn figure wearing a miter and ankle-length undergarment. The bishop near me, sensing trouble, turned and grabbed the cope. Frantically we fastened the snaps. To my immense relief, the scene came to an end as a celestial voice welcomed the souls of the departed heretics into heaven.

The night of my debut, the Met makeup artist, Victor Callegari, came to the super dressing room to transform me into a character from an El Greco painting. Now ascetic and fanatical looking, I seemed just right for an *auto-da-fé*.

At 9 p.m. the supers went downstairs to the stage. For the first time a wooden staff with a gold cross on top was handed to me. In the presence of a towering portrait of the Emperor Charles V, I paced back and forth backstage, with the cross-staff in my right hand, using my left hand to keep the cope from getting underfoot.

The scene prior to mine concluded, and the stage was transformed into a vast Madrid square. In the wings, a soldier asked me to hold his halberd while he adjusted his mustache. In turn, I asked him to hold my gold cross-staff while I placed the miter on my head.

I remembered to take off my glasses, check the snaps and newly-added safety pins on my cope and to adjust the rubber bands holding up my pants cuff.

From on stage a herald summoned us. Our procession of church dignitaries came down the cathedral steps and entered the square. As we moved across the stage, the eyes of the audience and our fellow performers were upon us. I felt as if I were in a dream. The cosmic events about to take place around me — Don Carlo (Placido Domingo) pleading on behalf of the persecuted people of Flanders; his drawing a sword against his father, King Phillip II, and being disarmed by Rodrigo, his closest friend — did not intrude on my dreamlike state. Here I was, having earlier in the day been practicing law in New York City, now performing on the stage of the Metropolitan Opera in 16th-century Madrid, enveloped in the glorious music of Verdi and the splendid voices on stage.

The scene ended with the principals, chorus and supers, about 200 of us, looking heavenward as the offstage celestial voice joyfully received the souls of the departed heretics. A worker high above the stage acknowledged our reverent gazes by waving back. Down came the curtain to thunderous applause.

Within seconds of the curtain's descent, stagehands rushed on to begin dismantling the set in preparation for the next act. The principals had moved downstage for curtain calls. I was slow in leaving. A stagehand brought me back to reality: "Bishop, I can't wait for you all day."

My debut had been a success. Even a critical success, with Andrew Porter writing in "The New Yorker" that in the *auto-da-fé* scene, "There is no stinting on supers."

I appeared in seven additional "Don Carlo" performances without mishap. The final performance was televised live to Europe, and later telecast in the United States.

For supers, the big money is in television. On this occasion, the usual supernumerary fee of $10 a performance soared to $153.23, minus $15 deducted by management as the first payment toward a $600 initiation fee for membership in the American Federation of Television and Radio Artists. (At this writing, I remain in arrears to AFTRA for the balance.)

It had been my intention to retire as a supernumerary after "Don Carlo", since nothing could match the grandeur of this opera nor the magnificence of my bishop's costume. But each time I pass the Metropolitan Opera House and recall the magic that takes place within, my resolve weakens. I may yet return to the stage of my triumph.

[1984]

WRITING

Enriching the Spirit

The Greeks had it right: Try, on a daily basis, to exercise the mind and body and enrich the spirit.

I exercise the mind through my work as a lawyer. As for exercising the body, I play basketball three times a week at a gymnasium — a word of Greek origin.

As for the spirit, writing gives me enormous pleasure. I gained the confidence to write in my mid-forties by undertaking, with a friend, a well-received book on urban environmental issues. Once you begin writing, it is difficult to stop. As Montaigne notes, "I have taken a road along which I shall continue…as long as there is ink and paper in the world."

Writing in longhand does have a disadvantage. Ink stains. "How does this happen?" asks the laundry man, looking at my shirts. "Writing," I respond. I carry these ink stains as a badge of honor.

Turgenev's mother understood the risks of writing. She warned her son, "I cannot comprehend your desire to become a writer! Is that an activity for a gentleman? ….A gentleman should serve the state and forge a career and a name for himself in that service, instead of blackening paper." And blackening yourself, she might have added. (Turgenev seems to have shared my preference for black ink.)

My encounters with the arts in New York City enrich my spirit.

Viewing Rembrandt's etching "Six's Bridge" at the Morgan Library and Museum, I see a landscape I know well, having spent time bicycling in Holland. The etching was undertaken, according to E.F. Gersaint, an 18th century Paris art dealer, "against time for a wager at the country house of his friend, Jan Six, while the servant was fetching the mustard, that had been forgotten for a meal, from the neighboring village."

The events surrounding that day must have given Rembrandt great pleasure. The company of Jan Six, a good friend who was a merchant, playwright and later, burgomaster of Amsterdam; a wager lightheartedly entered into; a delightful setting to work — "an open landscape that breathes the bright and windy seaside atmosphere of Holland," writes Jakob Rosenberg of the etching in his book "Rembrandt, Life and Work".

The scene depicted by Rembrandt has the quiet, unhurried feel of a Sunday afternoon. Perhaps it was also on a Sunday in 1874 when Manet painted Monet and his wife and son, at the same time Monet was painting Manet at his easel. (I came upon the Manet painting, "The Monet Family in Their Garden at Argenteuil," on a Sunday afternoon visit to the Metropolitan Museum of Art.) Later that day, Renoir joined them. Borrowing paint, brushes and canvas, he placed himself next to Manet to paint Monet. Friends serving as subjects, enjoying each other's company as they work.

Literature enriches the spirit. Early in 1894, Oscar Wilde's handwritten manuscript of his play "An Ideal Husband" arrived at Mrs. Marshall's Type Writing agency in London, perhaps brought there by Wilde himself.

"Mrs. Marshall can be relied on," he wrote years later. The Wilde manuscript is in the Morgan Library.

My favorite passage from the play. Lord Goring: "All I do know is that life cannot be understood without much charity, cannot be lived without much charity." Wisdom for every judge in the land.

This was Mrs. Marshall's second most interesting assignment, the first being when she typed "The Importance of Being Earnest" from Wilde's handwritten manuscript.

On Sunday walks in New York City, I sometimes end up at the Battery to look upon the harbor and at passing ships. I am part of a tradition going back at least as far as Herman Melville, for in "Moby-Dick" Melville writes of crowds gathering along the Battery to gaze out to sea, seeking respite from their lives "pent up in lathe and plaster — tied to counters, nailed to benches, clinched to desks."

On Mondays I return to the office to sit "clinched" to my desk

Each day my city affords me ample opportunities to enrich the spirit. [2008]

In the Writing Good Things Come

Samuel Johnson once said that a man can write anywhere or anytime "if he will set himself *doggedly* to it."

In addition to determination, I would include three other prerequisites for writing: having a degree of leisure time, what Boswell calls "ease and elbow-room" for the mind; catching hold of an idea, or at least the glimmer of an idea for a subject — plunge ahead urges Joyce, for "In the writing the good things will come"; and having an implement with which to perform the physical act of writing.

Concerning the last, I use a fountain pen. To apply pen directly to paper makes me feel part of a centuries-old literary tradition.

Needing only a legal-size pad – we lawyers use nothing else – enables me to write anywhere. First drafts I generally do at home on a table that serves the dual purpose of eating and writing, often with an opera playing in the background to provide inspiration. (At this very moment, it is the Saturday afternoon Metropolitan Opera radio broadcast of Donizetti's "L'Elisir d'Amore".)

An unlikely spot for making revisions is the Metropolitan Opera House itself. Just beneath the gold ceiling and raised chandeliers are small desks equipped with lamps. Here opera lovers and music students can follow the score at a performance. A fine place to work on an article during lengthy opera intermissions.

Park benches are wonderful places for writing. Especially Battery Park at the southern tip of Manhattan, with its harbor views of white-topped slapping waves and passing ships.

I have favorite spots abroad for writing. One is the terrace of friends who own a lovely villa in the south of France overlooking the Mediterranean Sea. When I visit them, I glance up from my papers to search the horizon for the white steamer setting forth across the shimmering sea on its daily voyage from Nice to Corsica.

Any location in Venice encourages writing. This is because writing comes more easily if one has gestated a piece in advance. The best way for me to do this is by taking long walks. Venice, like New York, is a wonderful walking city.

Keats, when he had gone to the Isle of Wight to work on "Endymion," came upon a picture of Shakespeare in the passageway of his rooming house. As Walter Jackson Bate writes in his eloquent biography of Keats, the landlady allowed him to move the picture into his room, where, after taking down a print of a French ambassador, he hung it above his books. Though he stayed at the rooming house only a week, the landlady insisted that he take the picture with him. Wherever Keats wrote, he always kept it by him.

God bless his landlady, Mrs. Cook. By her generous act, she served literature in a way few have ever done.

[1988]

Subway Rider, Writer

Writing can be a lonely activity. I enjoy writing in public spaces. One of my favorite is the New York City subway. Here I find no shortage of company.

Rush-hour trains are not desirable. It is not easy to write standing up with a neighbor's elbow in your face. By midmorning, things are calmer.

I do not travel on subways for the purpose of writing. Rather, writing is an activity I undertake when going from place to place on business or for pleasure. Like Thoreau, all I need are paper and pencil. (The family pencil business supplied Thoreau with plenty of pencils.)

The interiors of subway cars are surprisingly quiet, and the movement of the train is smooth as it speeds along steel rails. I have no trouble concentrating on a subway; indeed, I sometimes miss my stop. This is not true of buses and taxis. The potholes on city streets result in a bumpy ride, and concentration suffers.

Subways, however, are not without problems: like conductors who disturb the quiet by imparting too much information, and defective train announcement systems that produce ear-splitting sounds. When encountering either, I change trains.

The sounds of words are important to me. As I revise a piece, I like to read it aloud. Mumblers instill disquiet among fellow passengers. Not infrequently, the person next to me moves to another part of the car.

This piece is being written on a Lexington Avenue subway as the train travels uptown beneath crowded city streets. I glance out the window; there is no view to distract me, only the dark, gritty bleakness of a subway tunnel.

I had planned to write another paragraph, but the subway is approaching the station near where I live. The time has come to conclude this piece and vacate my writing room. Adieu.

[1998]

For Chekhov, It Was as Easy as Eating Pancakes

Saturday afternoon I sit at a table to write, but on what subject? Nothing comes to mind. Unlike Herman Melville, I have no "condor's quill" at the ready, no "Vesuvius' crater for an inkstand."

Writing came easily to Chekhov, "just the way I eat pancakes," he wrote. In his short stories, he portrayed less successful writers, like the one advised by his editor to save on postage by not submitting further drivel.

For Flaubert, writing was not easy. "Human language is like a cracked kettle on which we beat out tunes for bears to dance to, while all the time we long to move the stars to pity." ("Madame Bovary")

Many of the best writers experience difficulties. Here, in his journal for 1855, Thoreau evaluates his work: "Playing with words, — getting the laugh, — not always simple, strong, and broad."

This is Whitman's advice to himself as he prepared the second edition of "Leaves of Grass": "Make no puns/ funny remarks/Double entendres/'witty' remarks/ironies/ Sarcasms/Only that which/ is simply earnest/meant, — harmless/to any one's feelings/–unadorned/unvarnished...."

Chekhov set high goals for himself: "(1) absolute objectivity; (2) truth in the description of people and things; (3) maximum brevity; (4) boldness and originality; (5) compassion."

Informed by these writers, and their biographers — ("Chekhov" by Henri Troyat, "The Days of Henry Thoreau", by Walter Harding, and Justin Kaplan's "Walt Whitman, a Life") — I reach for pen and paper, ready to try again. [2002]

The Editor Sends His Regrets

Writing requires perseverance. The path, even of great writers, is often strewn with rejection slips.

In his short story "My Jubilee," Chekhov portrays a character who whimsically offers to celebrate the termination of his writing career on having just received his second thousandth rejection.

Chekhov had his own share of turndowns. They came, not by mail, but in the "Letter Box," the magazine section where editors commented on submissions. Ernest J. Simmons in "Chekhov, a Biography", writes how "With cold, trembling fingers he turned the pages to the fine print of their 'Letter Box' sections and ran his eye expectantly over comments to would-be authors."

Many of the comments directed to Chekhov were not encouraging. "A few witty words cannot obliterate such woefully insipid verbiage." "You have ceased to flower; you are withering. A pity. But no one can write without maintaining a critical attitude to his work."

These bruising remarks make the editors I deal with seem gentle by comparison. Harrison Salisbury, the founding editor of the Op-Ed page at "The New York Times", sent charming rejection notes. In his response to a labored piece of mine on Hans Sachs, hero of Wagner's "Die Meistersinger", Salisbury wrote: "Sorry — it's no sale on Sachs!" He published my first contribution and rejected the second. When turning down the third, he wrote: "Well, gosh – I guess the old average takes a beating — down to .333. But keep trying."

Other rejection notes stung, although, in retrospect they seem faintly amusing. "We found your essay to take an interesting point of view; that point is not quite proven by the manuscript." "Really, there's no over-arching theme. What did you have in mind?" "A self-addressed, stamped envelope should accompany all submissions."

Chekhov did not become one of the greatest writers by receiving only rejection slips. Hundreds of his stories were published. The "Letter Box" comment he may have appreciated most is the following, which appeared in the St. Petersburg humor weekly "Dragonfly" while he was still a medical student at Moscow University: "Not at all bad. Will print what was sent. Our blessings on your further efforts."

Rejections make the joy of acceptance all the greater. How many times have I stood on freezing-cold street corners late at night by a newsstand waiting for the first edition of "The New York Times" to arrive, and then with excitement and pride, turned the pages to find my piece.

In this respect, Dickens and I are comrades. Edgar Johnson writes in "Charles Dickens, His Tragedy and Triumph": "On a December evening, just before closing time, Dickens stepped into a bookshop on the Strand and asked for a new number of the Monthly Magazine. Would his piece be there? A little birdlike shopman gave him a copy from the counter; Dickens turned aside to glance hastily and nervously through the pages. There it was! … 'in all the glory of print.' So agitated that he wished only to be alone, he turned out of the crowded Strand and strode down the pavement of Whitehall to take refuge in Westminster Hall from the eyes of pedestrians. There for half an hour he paced the stone floor '[his] eyes so dimmed with pride and joy that they could not bear the street, and were not fit to be seen.' "

Alas, few writers are Chekhov or Dickens. For those of us who are not, perseverance is all the more necessary. "Through good report and through ill report, …through sunshine and through moonshine," in Poe's words, "we continue to toil. Nothing hurts our curiosity or our hope."

[1988]

The Best Companion for a Writer

As they toiled, each of the Gospel writers had a companion. In Renaissance paintings, Matthew, an angel; Luke, a bull; John, an eagle; and Mark, a lion.

At the Gallerie dell'Accademia, that treasure house of Venetian painting, there are four ceiling panels of the Gospel writers painted by Titian.

An angel stands behind the seated Matthew. Writing is a solitary undertaking, so Matthew benefits from both the companionship of the angel and the inspiration that it presumably imparts. What more could a writer want?

On the other hand, the angel's presence could be a distraction. Writers choose to work undisturbed for a reason. Worse still, what if the angel has a fondness for editing? To have an angel-editor peer over your shoulder, scrutinizing your every word, would be intolerable.

In the sacristy of the Church of San Sebastiano in Venice, Paolo Veronese has also painted the Gospel writers at work. Luke is making good use of the bull as a desktop. He has placed his book on the animal's flank.

Here again there is a downside. A restless bull means a moving writing surface, and there are considerable expenses related to the care and feeding of a bull.

Elsewhere in Venice, on a chapel wall in the Church of San Zaccaria is a 15th century painting depicting John the Evangelist. John "stands with an absorbed look sharpening a quill which he appears to have plucked from the disgruntled eagle at his feet," writes Hugh Honour in "The Companion Guide to Venice". (Nearby, Luke scratches his ear with yet another quill. That poor eagle!)

No writer wants to spend time with a sulking eagle. And no writer uses a quill today anyway. So John's eagle seems eminently dispensable.

But not — in my opinion — Mark's lion. A lion is useful for keeping bothersome people away. And this lion is a reader. What every writer wants. He holds a book with his paw. The open page reads, "Peace be unto you, Mark, my Evangelist."

For my writing companion, I would choose the literate lion. [2006]

LITERATURE

Literature and Travel

In 1959, three important events occurred in my life: I graduated from college where I had spent four years reading literature; I was introduced to the world of foreign travel; and I began Columbia Law School.

In Rome in the summer of that year, my college roommate and I stayed at a pensione near the Spanish Steps, by the house where John Keats died. At the time I remember reading one of his marvelous letters, in which he looked forward to a walking tour in the north of England and Scotland that will "make a sort of Prologue to the Life I intend to pursue — that is to write, to study and to see all Europe at the lowest expense. I will clamber through the Clouds and exist."

The letter pierced my heart. Here we were, a similar age, both filled with hope and vigor for the future, with a shared goal "to see all Europe," and with the same practical consideration, "at the lowest expense." But I knew, as he did not when he wrote this letter, that his would be a short life.

If travel is a delightful branch of learning, law school assuredly is not. During long hours spent in classes on evidence, civil procedure and real estate, my mind wandered, as Keats's had when a student at Guy's Hospital, London, though his mental wanderings were far more poetic: "The other day…during the lecture, there came a sunbeam into the room, and with it a whole troop of creatures floating in the ray; and I was off with them to Oberon and fairyland."

Practicing law, as I came to learn, requires hard work, rigorous thinking, discipline, close attention to detail and an ability to cope with client demands and never-ending deadlines. This is the Spartan life of lawyers.

But let's not forget the Athenians who placed a high premium on enriching the spirit. Consciously or not, more than fifty years ago I made a decision when leaving college, having been elated by immersion in literature, followed by the thrilling experience of foreign travel, to embrace literature and travel as essential parts of my life, whatever the future might bring.

Let me share with you two literary experiences flowing from my travels. The first concerns Keats, the second, Tolstoy.

In the Athenian spirit, I returned to Rome and to the Spanish Steps and the second floor room Keats occupied at 26 Piazza di Spagna.

Keats and his devoted companion, the painter Joseph Severn, reached Rome on November 15, 1820. Another English winter might prove fatal for him. Rome's far milder climate perhaps would be beneficial.

The room Keats occupied remains essentially as it was in his day, with a patterned ceiling, tile floor and windows overlooking the piazza and the Spanish Steps.

In "Posthumous Keats, a Personal Biography", Stanley Plumly writes: From his bedroom window "He can…lean out and look up at the dominating perspective of the church SS. Trinità dei Monti, which looms at the top of the 130 steps; or he can look down, to the left, at Bernini's Barcaccia — Old Boat — fountain [in the piazza], sinking day and night in its perpetual pale green waters." At night, Keats hears the calming waters of the fountain.

Keats purchases Italian books with a view to studying the language. He climbs the Spanish Steps and takes walks in the gardens of the Pincio. He rides horseback, though at a "snail-pace," according to Severn, as far as the Coliseum.

Here is Keats in the most beautiful part of Rome, in what chronologically should have been the prime of his life, but he is dying. To his close friend, Charles Brown, Keats wrote in his last letter: "I have an habitual feeling of my real life having passed, and that I am leading a posthumous existence. God knows how it would have been — but it appears to me — however, I will not speak of that subject.... I can scarcely bid you good-bye, even in a letter. I always made an awkward bow."

Following an eight week period of confinement to his room, Keats died on February 23, 1821, at the age of twenty-five. From his room I go to the Non-Catholic Cemetery by Rome's ancient wall, near the Pyramid of Gaius Cestius, where Keats is buried.

In the preface to "Adonais," his elegy on Keats, Shelley describes the burial place as "an open space among the ruins, covered in winter with violets and daisies." Keats's friends selected these words for his gravestone: "Here lies One/Whose Name was writ in Water."

A robust epitaph would have been far more suitable, for as Mr. Plumly points out, what killed Keats was "A disease of the lungs, not the heart and mind." Perhaps these lines of Keats:

But, when I am consumèd in the fire,
Give me new Phoenix wings to fly at my desire.

* * *

My visit to Tolstoy's country estate, Yasnaya Polyana, located south of Moscow, was a third-generation visit. In 1909, grandfather spent several days with Tolstoy to record his voice for a gramophone company represented by grandfather in Russia. Mother visited decades later.

The house is modest. The dining room table is set. Grandfather described the food as very plain. Close by is a small table with a lamp. After dinner, guests and family would sit around the table as Tolstoy read passages from his most recent work. In Tolstoy's study I come upon his writing desk and the gramophone grandfather presented to him.

Tolstoy lies buried in a birch wood not far from the house. I walk to the grave in a gentle rain, called "a mushroom rain" by Russians. There is no monument, only an earth mound covered with leaves.

When a child, Tolstoy had been told a story by his brother, Nicholas, that made a profound impression on him. Late in life Tolstoy wrote, "I used to believe that there was a green stick on which words were carved that would destroy all the evil in the hearts of men and bring them everything good, and I still believe today that there is such a truth, that it will be revealed to men, and will fulfill its promise."

In his 82nd year, Tolstoy was buried where he believed the green stick lay.

* * *

How immeasurably literature and travel have enriched my life. [2009]

Chekhov by My Desk

On the office wall by my desk, I have placed a photograph of Lincoln — for a lawyer, not an unusual choice. Next to Lincoln is a photograph of Anon Pavlovich Chekhov. Few visitors recognize him. He is my favorite writer.

Tolstoy and Turgenev came from privileged backgrounds. Not so Chekhov, whose father was born a serf and did not obtain freedom until age 16. Chekhov wrote of himself as being "a young man, the son of a serf…who was whipped many times…who used his fists and tormented animals…who was hypocritical in his dealings with God and men gratuitously, out of the mere consciousness of his insignificance — write [he tells an aspiring writer] how this youth squeezes the slave out of himself drop by drop, and how, waking up one fine morning, he feels that in his veins flows no longer the blood of a slave but that of a real man…." (Solzhenitsyn believed that every Russian living under Stalinist rule needed, as Chekhov had done, to squeeze "the slave out of himself drop by drop.")

Throughout his life, Chekhov helped poor people, providing medical treatment to peasants, assisting in famine relief and donating money and books to schools. Chekhov's

Last Will and Testament concludes with these words: "Help the poor. Look after mother. All of you live in peace."

In living out his own life, what an extraordinary contrast Chekhov was to the passivity of so many of the figures in his short stories and plays. As an example, at age 30, enjoying the comforts of Moscow and literary recognition, Chekhov chose to undertake a long and difficult journey across Russia to the Pacific coast to visit the penal colony on Sakhalin Island. In this letter, he explains to his publisher why he is making the journey:

> I haven't even left yet, but thanks to the books I've had to read, I've learned about things that everyone should know on pain of forty lashes and that I had the ignorance not to know before.... You write that Sakhalin is of no use or interest to anyone. Is that really so? Sakhalin could be of no use or interest only to a society that doesn't deport thousands of people to it and doesn't spend millions on it....

Chekhov spent three months on Sakhalin, conducting a medical census of prisoners. He wrote of his book based on these experiences, "It gives me joy that this harsh convict's robe shall have a place in my literary wardrobe."

I visit New York State prisons. This passage, from Chekhov's short story, "The Murder," about a Sakhalin convict, would evoke a sad, strong sense of recognition from prisoners I meet:

> He looked with strained eyes into the darkness, and it seemed to him that through the thousand miles of that mist he could see

> home.... His eyes were dimmed with tears; but still he gazed into the distance where the pale lights of the steamer faintly gleamed, and his heart ached with yearning for home, and he longed to live, to go back home to tell them of his new faith and to save from ruin if only one man, and to live without suffering if only for one day.

Chekhov lists "compassion" as one of his aesthetic tenets. In his short story "An Attack of Nerves," he writes of someone, "There are all sorts of talents — talent for writing, talent for the stage, talent for art; but he had — peculiar talent a talent for humanity." As did Chekhov.

This passage from the short story, "Gooseberries," conveys Chekhov's humane concerns, "themes old but not yet out of date":

> But we do not see and we do not hear those who suffer, and what is terrible in life goes on somewhere behind the scenes....It's a case of general hypnotism. There ought to be behind the door of every happy, contented man some one standing with a hammer continually reminding him with a tap that there are unhappy people; that however happy he may be, life will show him her claws sooner or later, trouble will come for him — disease, poverty, losses, and no one will see or hear, just as now he neither sees nor hears others.

In Chekhov's short stories and plays, there are unhappy people from all classes, not just the poor, deserving of our sympathy. They find life difficult to live, like those in "The Cherry Orchard" who are unable to adjust to changing times. Liubov Andryeevna here bids farewell to the just-sold family estate: "Oh my darling, my precious, my beautiful orchard! My life, my youth, my happiness... goodbye!... Goodbye!"

Chekhov extends his sympathy to each of them.

Ernest J. Simmons writes in "Chekhov, A Biography" that even "with all his acute insight, Tolstoy never quite perceived the breadth and tolerance of Chekhov's judgment, his tenderness for those who suffered, or his charity in the face of forgivable weakness." Chekhov himself wrote that "An author must be humane to his finger tips."

Vershinin in "Three Sisters" captures Chekhov's sympathy for people entrapped by life, and also his quiet humor. "What shall I philosophize about now? ... [Laughs.] Yes, life is difficult. It seems quite hopeless for a lot of us, just a kind of impasse...."

"Three Sisters" conveys despair and courage, concluding with Masha's words: "We're left alone...to start our lives all over again. We must go on living...we must go on living." "Uncle Vanya" ends with these words of Sonia: "Well, what can we do? We must go on living! [A pause.] We shall go on living, Uncle Vanya."

Those of us who have a professional or official relation to the suffering of others — lawyers, judges, police officers, doctors, social workers — can benefit from reading Chekhov. He deepens our understanding of the human condition; a parlous condition, in his view.

Years ago, when I was in the Crimea, I visited Chekhov's house at Yalta. In poor health much of the time, he lived there to avoid the bitter cold of Moscow. In full-view of the desk where he wrote "Three Sisters" and "The Cherry Orchard", Chekhov had placed on the wall a large print of Alexander Pushkin. How pleased I was to find that Chekhov honored his literary hero in the same way I honor mine.

Postscript:

Chekhov is traveling alone by night train from Moscow to St. Petersburg to visit his ill brother, Alexander. He writes in a letter: "Generally, a vile night.... My only consolation was my darling precious Anna (I mean Karenina) who kept me busy all the way."

Chekhov and Tolstoy sharing the same railway carriage: a favorite moment for me in literature. [2009]

A Chekhov Bookworm in New York

Having arranged a series of three seminars on the short stories of Chekhov at the New York Society Library, I am making use of every available moment, day and night, to read the assigned stories lest I disgrace myself at the sessions being conducted by a distinguished Chekhov scholar.

Reading Chekhov on the Subway. A crowded subway car presents many distractions. A man boards holding a collection of large balloons. Barely visible behind his balloons, he is delivering them to a celebratory event somewhere in the city. A boy shins up a pole in the subway car. A cyclist boards. He prefers rail travel to pedaling to his destination. The train leaves the dark tunnel to cross the Manhattan Bridge to Brooklyn. From the subway car window, views of the East River, Brooklyn Bridge and Lower Manhattan. Alas, Anton Pavlovich, I am making little headway in reading your short stories.

Reading Chekhov at Work. Forget it. Too many distractions. But I do look at the Chekhov picture by my desk.

Reading Chekhov in Central Park. I watch a weekend softball game. Beyond the outfield, the glorious Fifth Avenue and Central Park South skyline provided by the Pierre, Sherry-Netherland, Hampshire House and Essex House hotels. As a late afternoon sun casts a golden glow over the city, I read aloud in the stands this Chekhov passage: "And he was charmed with the evening, the farmhouses and villas on the road, and the birch trees, and the quiet atmosphere all around, when the fields and woods and the sun seemed preparing, like the workpeople now on the eve of the holiday, to rest, and perhaps to pray...."

Reading Chekhov at a Concert. My brother-in-law and nephew are singing works by Schumann and Stravinsky. As they sing, I pretend to follow the libretto while surreptitiously reading Chekhov.

Reading Chekhov in Chinatown. I am having lunch at Maria's. Chinese is spoken all around me. At the table, I read aloud passages from Chekhov.

Reading Chekhov at Home. I lie on the couch in my favorite position — horizontal — and fall asleep.

Postscript.

Despite obstacles, distractions and human weakness, I complete the 19 assigned Chekhov short stories and perform creditably at the seminar sessions.

Ah Chekhov, you who understand how difficult life is for most people. You who are generous in portraying those who strive to live a better life, even when they fail, which we mostly do. You who are modest, who never condemns. You who are tender toward those who suffer. [2003]

Thoreau's Path in New York City

My admiration for Thoreau is unbounded. For his life of independence. For his greatness as a writer.

Imagine my surprise and delight to learn that this quintessential man of the country, this "self-appointed inspector of snow-storms and rain-storms...surveyor, if not of highways, than of forest paths...." Spent time in that most urban of places. New York — my city.

Thoreau traveled from Concord to New York at least seven times during his life. Some of his trips were in connection with the pencil business that his family owned.

On his trips to New York, Thoreau acted like any other tourist. He walked along Fifth Avenue, admiring the houses, and went to museums, where he saw "sculptures and paintings innumerable." He made frequent visits to Barnum's Museum. There he came upon a herd of giraffes, referred to in his "Journal" as "camelopards." He browsed in "antique" bookstores along Fulton Street in Lower Manhattan. He attended the opera. Being Thoreau, in the midst of all this bustle, he managed to spot a muskrat swimming across a pool of water.

Thoreau's stays in the city usually were of a few days' duration, except for his second visit, in 1843, when he stayed from May to December. He had come to New York to tutor Ralph Waldo Emerson's young nephews, with whose family he lived on Staten Island, and to explore possible writing opportunities with publishers.

He enjoyed walking around Staten Island. A few days after his arrival in the spring of 1843, he wrote home: "I have already run over no small part of the island, to the highest hill, and some way along the shore. From the hill directly behind the house I can see New York. Brooklyn, Long Island, the Narrows, through which vessels bound to and from all parts of the world chiefly pass.... Far in the horizon there was a fleet of sloops bound up the Hudson, which seemed to be going over the edge of the earth...."

He loved the sea, describing it as "very solitary and remote." He saw men drag their boats up on the sand with oxen. He saw "great shad nets spread to dry, crabs and horse-shoes crawling over the sand." Now he heard the roar of the sea, "and not the wind in Walden woods."

To his sister, Sophia, Thoreau wrote of the trees and flowers on Staten Island. The fields were fragrant from the aroma of cedar. He admired the tulip trees. The woods were filled with honeysuckle. The season was far more advanced than in Concord. By May, "The apricots growing out of doors are already as large as plums. The apple, pear, peach, cherry and plum trees, have shed their blossoms."

But Staten Island was not New York City. Only in 1898 did it become a borough of the city, and to this day it remains a far different place from Manhattan. While Thoreau could relate to rural Staten Island, he found New York City a less congenial place.

To Emerson, he wrote, "I don't like the city better, the more I see it, but worse." And to his mother: "I do not like their cities and forts, with their morning and evening guns, and sails flapping in one's eye. I want a whole continent to breathe in, and a good deal of solitude and silence, such as all Wall Street cannot buy, — nor Broadway with its wooden pavement."

Because, as Thoreau wrote to Emerson during this period, he always sought to be "as much the pupil as I can be," he used his time in New York to see a great deal of the city. Thoreau shared one thing in common with New Yorkers: He loved to walk. He walked along the same avenues — those great arteries of the city — that I walk along today, and on those avenues he saw some of the same buildings that I see today. He saw the same rivers that I see, though none then were spanned by bridges. He saw the sun set over the Hudson River.

For me, each walk along the streets, each sight of familiar buildings, each view of the city's rivers binds me closer to my city. But for Thoreau, the city never took hold of his heart. In New York he remained a man of Concord, just as I, when visiting Concord, remain a New Yorker. He wrote to his family, "I carry Concord ground in my boots and in my hat, — and am I not made of Concord dust?"

Homesick, and with not much to show from his pursuit of publishers, Thoreau left New York City to return to Concord in mid-December, 1843. Nineteen months later he moved to Walden Pond. His cabin on Walden Pond is the size of my apartment bedroom. [1992]

Whitman

Some authors are associated in our minds with particular cities. Think of London and you think of Dickens; Paris, Balzac; Dublin, Joyce; St. Petersburg, Dostoevsky.

And New York? Whitman.

Justin Kaplan, in his biography "Walt Whitman, A Life", points out that "America's first urban poet began as a student of the city's rhythms and sounds." In 1830, at age eleven, Whitman's formal studies ended and he started work as an office boy in a law firm, exploring the two cities along the East River — New York and Brooklyn. Among those to whom he delivered legal papers was Aaron Burr. "He had a way," wrote Whitman, "of giving me a bit of fruit on these occasions — an apple or a pear."

As a newspaperman and poet, Whitman came to know his two cities well. "Brooklyn of ample hills was mine,/I too walk'd the streets of Manhattan Island...." He enjoyed riding the Broadway omnibus and would help the drivers collect fares. On the omnibus, or on the East River ferry boats plying between Brooklyn and New York, Whitman sometimes declaimed Homer and Shakespeare, or sang snatches from opera. He loved the opera and believed that without the emotional intensity it provided him, he might never have become a poet.

The harbor was a favorite part of the city for Whitman. The first time he ever wanted to write anything enduring was "when I saw a ship under full sail, and had the desire to describe it exactly as it seemed to me." And describe ships he did, with lines such as these, written later: "Look'd toward the lower bay to notice the vessels arriving, .../ Saw the white sails of schooners and sloops, saw the ships at anchor,/The sailors at work in the rigging or out astride the spars,/The round masts, the swinging motion of the hulls, the slender serpentine pennants...."

As Whitman traveled by foot, omnibus and ferry, he became increasingly aware of the beauty of his island cities — New York and Brooklyn. "The glories strung like beads on my smallest sights and hearings, on the walk in the street and the passage over the river."

In the streets of New York, he was witness to historical events. "When a great event happens, or the news of some great solemn thing spreads out among the people, it is curious to go forth and wander a while in the public ways." At age 14, he saw President Andrew Jackson ride through the city streets in an open carriage. (Whitman's 72 years, 1819-1892, overlapped the lives of John Adams, Jefferson, Jackson, Lincoln and Franklin Roosevelt — a reminder of the brevity of our nation's history.)

By City Hall, near the spot where, in the presence of General George Washington the Declaration of

Independence was read to the Continental Army five days after its adoption in Philadelphia, Whitman watched President-elect Lincoln arrive at the Astor House. "I had…a capital view of it all, and especially of Mr. Lincoln, his look and gait — his perfect composure and coolness — his unusual and uncouth height, his dress of complete black, stovepipe hat push'd back on the head, dark-brown complexion, seam'd and wrinkled yet canny-looking face…. [F]our sorts of genius, four mighty and primal hands, will be needed to the complete limning of this man's future portrait — the eyes and brains and finger-touch of Plutarch and Eschylus and Michel Angelo, assisted by Rabelais."

Whitman learned of the firing upon Fort Sumter when walking down Broadway to the Brooklyn ferry to return home after attending a performance of Verdi's "A Masked Ball" at the Academy of Music on 14th Street. Newsboys were selling papers announcing the event. He bought a paper and read it under a gas street lamp.

He shared the excitement of his fellow New Yorkers when word reached the city of the meeting between General Ulysses Grant and Robert E. Lee at Appomattox Courthouse, bringing to a close the Civil War.

Church bells tolled six days later, this time for the slain President Lincoln. Jubilant banners along Broadway were replaced by weepers of black muslin. Read one banner: "The silent city from its homes and towers/With universal tears flings out its signs/Of woe." As Whitman strode along Broadway that day, he wrote in his notebook: "Black clouds driving overhead. Lincoln's death — black, black, black — as you look toward the sky — long broad black like the great serpents."

For Dickens, Balzac, Joyce and Dostoevsky, their city served as a source of inspiration. The same was true for Whitman. The people, streets, events, rivers and harbor of this "Proud and passionate city — mettlesome, mad, extravagant city" contributed to his greatness as a poet.

[1990]

Thoreau and Whitman Meet in Brooklyn

On November 10, 1856, Henry David Thoreau called upon Walt Whitman at his home on Classon Avenue in the city of Brooklyn for their first and only meeting. "Walden" had been published in the summer of 1854, and the first edition of "Leaves of Grass" eleven months later. A coming together of two towering figures in American letters — the poet of the city and the prose-poet of the country side.

The two men shared much in common; for example, an inability to hold a steady job. Whitman's mother said of her son that he "had no business but going out and coming in to eat, drink, write, and sleep." Thoreau wrote of Whitman that he "has no employment but to read and write in the forenoon, and walk in the afternoon, like all the rest of the scribbling gentry." Thoreau's daily schedule exactly!

Both loved walking. As with Thoreau, Whitman's inspiration from his walks found its way into his writings, but unlike Thoreau, Whitman inhabited an urban landscape. Of "Leaves of Grass" he wrote, "Remember, the book arose out of my life in Brooklyn and New York...absorbing a million people...with an intimacy, an eagerness, an abandon, probably never equaled."

Both suffered acute writerly woes. Justin Kaplan notes in "Walt Whitman, a Life", that Whitman set in type pages of "Leaves of Grass" which "he also designed, produced, published, promoted (shamelessly, his critics said)...." Despite all efforts, few copies were sold. For Whitman, the one bright spot came with Emerson's letter in praise of "Leaves of Grass". "I find it the most extraordinary piece of wit & wisdom that America has yet contributed....I greet you at the beginning of a great career...."

A thousand copies of Thoreau's first book, "A Week on the Concord and Merrimack Rivers", had been printed. Four years later, a wagon from his Boston publisher arrived in Concord filled with unsold copies. "They are something more substantial than fame, as my back knows, which has borne them up two flights of stairs to a place similar to that to which they trace their origin....I have now a library of nearly nine hundred volumes, over seven hundred of which I wrote myself."

Both were men of uncompromising independence. Thoreau: "I would not have any one adopt my mode of living on any account; for, beside that before he has fairly learned it I may have found out another for myself. I desire that there may be as many different persons in the world as possible; but I would have each one be very careful to find out and pursue his own way...."

Whitman: "I had my choice when I commenc'd. I bid neither for soft eulogies, big money returns, nor the approbation of existing schools and conventions.... I have had my say entirely my own way...." Or more dramatically, "I sound my barbaric yawp over the roofs of the world."

When they met, Thoreau was 39 and Whitman 37. With them was Bronson Alcott, a close friend of Thoreau and Emerson.

From Alcott's Journals:

"He [Whitman] receives us kindly, yet awkwardly, and takes us up two narrow flights of stairs to sit or stand as we might in his attic study — also the bedchamber of himself and his feeble brother, the pressure of whose bodies was still apparent in the unmade bed standing in one corner, and the vessel scarcely hidden underneath.... Each seemed planted fast in reserves, surveying the other curiously — like two beasts, each wondering what the other would do, whether to snap or run...."

Ten days later, Thoreau wrote to a friend, "I am still somewhat in a quandary about him — feel that he is essentially strange to me, at any rate...."

When they met, Whitman gave Thoreau a copy of the second edition of "Leaves of Grass". A month after their meeting, Thoreau writes the same friend, "I have found this poem exhilarating encouraging.... On the whole it sounds to me very brave & American.... We ought to rejoice greatly in him."

As to the impact of "Leaves of Grass" on Thoreau's work, Robert D. Richardson, Jr. writes in "Henry Thoreau, A Life of the Mind" that Thoreau "responded to Whitman's tremendous capacity for joy, the quality of enthusiasm in which Emerson also responded.... Most important of all, Whitman's emphasis on intensity of experience and immediacy of communication coincided perfectly with

Thoreau's growing recognition of the central goal of intensity in his own writing."

And Thoreau may have influenced Whitman. A quarter century after Thoreau died at the age of 44 from tuberculosis, Whitman wrote of him: "One thing about Thoreau keeps him very near to me: I refer to his lawlessness — his dissent — his going his own absolute road let hell blaze all it chooses." [2007]

Volume 50

A commonplace book is a collection of literary passages and occasional thoughts, reflecting the interests of the compiler.

At law school I began the practice of writing down passages from my reading that had a special appeal to me. A half century later, I am launched on volume 50 of my commonplace book.

Impressed? Don't be. Compared to Emerson, I am moving at a snail's pace. Starting at age 17, he filled more than 200 notebooks over the next 50 years. He titled the first volume of his commonplace book "The Wide World No. 1." (Gogol called his, "Hold-All Notebook.")

When reading a book, I place pencil marks in the margin, and after completing it, go through it again, copying favorite passages into my commonplace book.

Why do I bother making this effort? Partly, to remember what has given me pleasure. Perhaps also to make important events less ephemeral, such as the reading of a book that has changed my life. As I have undertaken more writing in recent years, my commonplace book has become a treasure trove of ideas for new pieces.

For me, reading and rereading the entries in Central Park and elsewhere in the city is a delight. What I put down in 1962 gives me pleasure in 2012, my tastes not having changed that much over the years. (An indication, I hope, of early development, not stagnation.) At each reading, I encounter old friends.

Many of the entries in my commonplace book deal with governance and leadership, reflecting I believe, the best thinking and instincts of those who have been before us on the road.

Jefferson: "The great principles of right and wrong are legible to every reader; to pursue them requires not the aid of many counselors."

Washington: "It is not the part of a good citizen to despair of the republic."

Franklin: "I have long been accustomed to receive more blame as well as more praise, than I deserved. It is the lot of every public man, and I leave one account to balance the other."

Lincoln: "[T]o elevate the condition of men — to lift artificial weights from all shoulders; to clear the paths of laudable pursuit for all; to afford all an unfettered start and a fair chance in the race of life."

These other entries provide guidance to me in the difficult business of living life:

Tolstoy, in a letter to George Bernard Shaw: "Indeed, my dear Shaw, life is a great and serious business, and each of us must contrive, in the brief time we have been allotted, to discover what our job is and do that job as earnestly as we can."

Montaigne was a favorite of Captain Vere in Herman Melville's "Billy Budd". "He loved books," Melville writes of Vere, "never going to sea without a newly replenished library, compact but of the best." Montaigne appeals to Vere as one of those writers "who free from cant and convention, honestly and in the spirit of common sense philosophize upon realities."

Samuel Johnson: "We see a little, and form an opinion: we see more, and change it. This inconstancy and unsteadiness, to which we must so often find ourselves liable, ought certainly to teach us moderation and forbearance towards those who cannot accommodate themselves to our sentiments."

Keats sought to avoid dark moods when "any little vexation grows in five Minutes into a theme for Sophocles."

Primo Levi, the Italian writer, used this Yiddish proverb as an epigraph for the third volume of his autobiography, "The Periodic Table": "Troubles overcome are good to tell."

A number of entries are in my commonplace book for the great pleasure they give me:

January 1, 1500. Venice. Titian calling to Giorgione from the street: "Zorzo! Get up, Zorzo! Our century has begun!"

The philosopher Martin Buber: Men are "the brown-bread on whose crust I break my teeth, a bread of which I can never have enough.... Aye, those tousle-headed and good-for-nothings, how I love them."

Balzac to his sister: "Do you know, I've spent a whole week ruminating and broodulating and eatulating and strollulating without doing anything useful?"

The painter Joan Miró describing a visit, as a young man, to a museum in Barcelona: "There was a Monet landscape in that show. It was so beautiful that when the guard wasn't looking, I went over and kissed it."

Boswell is brooding on his failure to achieve success, either in law or politics. His 16-year-old son James writes to him: "Sir, do not suffer yourself to be melancholy. Think not on your having missed preferment.... [T]hey who have obtained places and pensions...have not the fame of having been the biographer of Johnson or the conscious exultation of a man of genius. They have not enjoyed your happy and convivial hours.... In short, would you rather than have enjoyed so many advantages have been a rich, though dull, plodding lawyer?"

Stendhal, on the first entry in his journal, makes a grammatical mistake. He is not concerned. "There will be a lot more, because I am making it a rule not to stand on ceremony and never to erase." [2012]

Book Selections of the Founding Fathers

On April 30, 1789, from the balcony of Federal Hall, George Washington took the oath of office as President of the United States. The president and Congress shared space with The New York Society Library in Federal Hall, located on the corner of Wall and Nassau Streets, when New York City was the nation's first capital.

The library had been founded in 1754 by a group of six young New Yorkers — five lawyers and a merchant — in the belief that "a Public Library would be very useful, as well as ornamental to this City...." In the view of one founder, New York lacked "a spirit of Inquiry among the people. It is indeed prodigious that in so populous a City... few Gentlemen have any relish for learning. Sensuality has devoured all greatness of soul and scarce one in a thousand is even disposed to talk serious."

Books were ordered from England. They included a "Life of Mahomet," the works of Milton and Locke, a history of France ("the best"), lives of Cromwell and Tsar Peter, "All Cicero's Works that are translated," and debates in Parliament.

In October 1754, the books arrived from England on the *Captain Miller*. With a library, New York now had an opportunity, the "New York-Mercury" editorialized, to "show that she comes not short of the other Provinces, in Men of excellent Genius who, by cultivating the Talents of Nature, will take off that Reflection cast on us by the neighbouring Colonies, of being an Ignorant People."

From 1774 to 1788, the library suspended operations. During the Revolutionary War, British soldiers stole library books in their knapsacks, not to read, but to barter for grog, or to tear up to make wadding for rifles. Six hundred books were hidden from the soldiers in St. Paul's Chapel blocks away. When the library re-opened in 1789, it had a collection of 3,100 books available as a resource to its 239 subscribing members, among them Alexander Hamilton, Aaron Burr and John Jay, and also available to the president and members of Congress. (Hence the library's claim to be the first Library of Congress.) Occupying a room on the top floor, the library was the only institution in Federal Hall not mandated by the U.S. Constitution.

The library's charging ledger for 1789-92, bound in leather and weighing 18 pounds, was misplaced for years and then found in 1934 in a trash pile in the basement of its fourth home at 109 University Place. (Since 1937, the library has been in its fifth home at 53 East 79th Street.) Today the ledger is a priceless possession, recording titles of books taken out and the names of borrowers. With care and excitement, I examine the pages of the library's charging ledger.

June 24, 1789. The first entry records that the Reverend Dr. Lynn borrowed "Animated Nature" by Oliver Goldsmith. Dr. Lynn served as chaplain to the Congress. He was fined seven pence for returning the book late.

July 31. "Elements of Criticism - 1 - Ovo. H. Vice-president-self." Shorthand for Vice-President John Adams himself appearing at the library to take out volume 1 of "Elements of Criticism" (octavo size), a philosophical work by Lord Henry Kames. Volume returned on Aug. 17.

Aug. 21. Volume 2 taken out by "Doork" for "H. Vice-President." This time, instead of personally coming to the library, the vice-president sent the doorkeeper to collect the second volume of "Elements of Criticism." There is no record of volume 2 being returned.

October 5. "Law of Nations [&] Commons Debates - volume 12 - President." Here the ledger records that President Washington took out "The Law of Nations" by Emmerich de Vattel. Also, volume 12 of the House of Commons Debates. There is no record of either volume being returned. (221 years later, in 2010, the chairmen and Librarian of George Washington's Mount Vernon Estate and Gardens returned to the library an identical copy of the Vattel work. In exchange, the New York Society Library forgave the late charges.)

Alexander Hamilton borrowed two novels, "The Amours of Count Palviano and Eleanora" and as recorded in the ledger, "Edward Mortimer (hist. of) by a lady."

In 1789, Aaron Burr took out "Revolutions in Geneva"; a volume of Swift; and "Decline and Fall of the Roman Empire" by Gibbon. In 1790, he turned to Voltaire, reading nine volumes and then to the 44 volumes making up the series, "An Unusual History," self-described as a history "from the earliest account of Time, compiled from original authors." His lighter reading included the novels, "Mysterious Husband" and "False Friend."

The New York Society Library charging ledger records books borrowed by Chief Justice John Jay. (On Feb. 1, 1790, in a building on Broad Street called the Exchange, the U.S. Supreme Court held its first session.) These books included:

Literature. The works of Jonathan Swift; "Don Quixote", Voltaire's, "Candidus," or "All For the Best," as the volume is noted in the ledger; "The Fair Syrian, a novel"; Frances Burney's, "Cecilla, or Memoirs of an Heiress"; "Arabian Nights Entertainments", consisting of one thousand and one stories, related by the Sultaness of the Indies"; and John Aubrey's, "Miscellanies," a collection of stories on ghosts and dreams.

History. Plutarch's, "Lives"; "Lives of the Admirals, and other Eminent British Seamen"; "The History of the Five Indian Nations of Canada"; "The History of the

Revolution of South Carolina, from a British Province to an Independent State"; and "An Essay on the Life of the Honorable Major-General Israel Putnam."

Travel. Captain James Cook's, "A Voyage towards the South Pole, and Round the World"; "A Tour through Sicily and Malta"; "Travels into Muscovy, Persia, and Parts of the East-Indies, containing an accurate description of whatever is most remarkable in those countries"; "A Voyage Round the World in the Years 1766-1769," by the Comte Louis Antoine de Bougainville; "A General Description of China, containing the topography of the fifteen provinces which compose this vast empire"; "Travels in Spain"; "Travels to Discover the Source of the Nile in 1768-1773"; and "Travels in North America in the Years 1780-1782", by the Marquis Francois Jean de Chastellux.

Science. Comte de Buffon's,"Natural History"; "Chambers', Cyclopaedia, or General Dictionary of Arts and Sciences"; and "Essays on the Intellectual Powers of Man."

Few of the books he borrowed from the New York Society Library are law-related. (The court doubtless had its own collection of law books.) What stands out when examining the library's charging ledger is both the breadth of the chief justice's interests and his wide reading in literature, history, travel and science.

May we be encouraged by his example to expand, through reading, our own horizons.

* * *

Some of the material used in this essay is drawn from "The New York Society Library, 250 Years," edited by Henry S.F. Cooper, Jr. and Jenny Lawrence, library trustees.

[2007]

PARTING

Timeless Tides in New York City

New York is a city in perpetual motion. Day and night, people and vehicles travel the streets; subways, trains and planes arrive and depart.

Yet daily we ignore a primal event occurring in our midst. An event making our daily rushing about seem insignificant. I speak of the tidal flows in and out of the city.

This very morning, high tide was at 8:51 a.m. While I was sleeping, and then dressing for work, and later walking through Central Park to the subway, 260 billion cubic feet of ocean water surged through the Narrows beneath the Verrazano–Narrows Bridge into the Upper Bay and along the shorelines of this city of islands.

The ocean water continues rushing up the Hudson River, causing this southern flowing river to reverse course and bringing salt seawater as far north as Poughkeepsie, with the tidal impact reaching all the way to Troy. Salt and fresh water meet, the fresh water emanating from Lake Tear of the Clouds in the Adirondacks, and from rivers, mountain streams and hundreds of creeks flowing into the Hudson.

Beneath the waters, scores of different fish mingle, including sturgeon and striped bass, both spawned in the river, both departing from the river for the sea, later to return to the river to continue the cycle of life.

By midafternoon the tidal waters will have receded. The next high tide will be at 9:03 p.m., as I finish dinner in my apartment.

The ebb and flow of the tides; the ebb and flow of daily life.

Another great tide impacts the city, far more visibly: the arrival of people from many lands.

In 1609, Henry Hudson navigated the river bearing his name. New Amsterdam was founded in 1625. Less than 30 years later, 18 languages were spoken in the city. Waves of immigrants arrived in the 19th century from Ireland, German, Italy and Eastern Europe.

The flow of newcomers continues. A diverse population has been a constant throughout the city's history. Today, people from nearly every land live in New York. Almost half the city's population is foreign-born.

Richard Holmes, in "Dr. Johnson & Mr. Savage", writes of Johnson's friendship with Richard Savage being "tidal like the River Thames; a friendship of arrivals and departures in the great city."

The flow of tides and people, arrivals and departures, in the past, now, and in the future. [2000]

Retirement Thoughts

Some lawyers choose a "Downtown death," where your secretary hears a thud, enters your office and finds you lifeless, face down on the desk, arms protectively extended over documents, having just completed, at age 100, the most important transaction of your career.

When I step down from my job as executive director of Volunteers of Legal Service, I will be 74; in China, 75, pursuant to natal calculations in China where you are deemed a year old at birth.

At my office, I open a new file, a manila folder marked "Future," and on a legal pad I have taken to compiling a list of opportunities. These are placed under one of two headings: "Reality" or "Fantasy."

Let me start with "Fantasy":

• Rise late each morning. After a breakfast of orange juice, a warm croissant and hot chocolate, repair to Central Park to sit on a bench in the sun and listen to songbirds. "Birdsong provided intimation of the music of heaven" to the French composer, Olivier Messiaen, noted a "New York Times" obituary writer.

• March up Fifth Avenue in a parade.

• Serve as United States consul in Venice. A namesake, the novelist William Dean Howells — no relation — did so. Howells was appointed consul by President Abraham Lincoln, having written a campaign biography for him. In my case, early on in 2008, I made the maximum contribution allowed an individual under the Federal Election Campaign Act to Barack Obama's campaign for president. (Mercifully, the limit then was $2,400.) I know Venice well. I would well represent U.S. interests there, whatever they are.

• If I can't be consul, work as a crew member on a tugboat in Venice. I have a fondness for tugs. The joy of escorting cruise ships. The bracing sea air.

• Serve as the Astronomer Royal of England. A holder of the position described his responsibilities: "The Astronomer Royal's duties are so exiguous that they could be performed posthumously."

Vaporous responsibilities, extending beyond the holder's lifetime, suggest the wisdom of moving on to opportunities under the heading, "Reality."

"I long to embrace; to include in my own short life," Chekhov wrote, "all that is accessible to man. I long to speak, to read, to wield a hammer in a great factory, to keep watch at sea, to plow."

In my 74 years, I have been a painter (creosoting cabins in Vermont), waiter, dairy farmhand, camp counselor and lawyer. And also traveler, writer and teacher. It is with these three last roles that my future may lie.

• Traveler. Travel is a joy of life. I have been privileged to travel a great deal, but there are many places I have not seen: China, Australia, New Zealand, Indonesia, Iran, Peru, Cuba, and in the United States, the south, the Pacific northwest and Alaska.

And I want to travel far more within my own city. Thoreau felt he could never come to know Concord completely. Though born, raised and practicing law here, I make no claim to knowing New York City. In truth, my knowledge is pretty much limited to Manhattan Island, south from 98th to the Battery. There are many neighborhoods for me to explore in the five boroughs; subway lines as yet untraveled, to travel; the cuisines of 180 lands to sample.

• Writer. Or I could spend my days writing, perhaps laying out on a gymnasium floor my published essays, columns and travel journals, numbering in the hundreds, and selecting the best for a collection of essays.

• Teacher. Or I might return to teaching. While at Columbia Law School, I taught sixth graders at St. Bernard's School and children in grades 4 to 8 in Puerto Rico.

I found teaching to be a thrilling experience. My students and I learned a lot together and laughed a lot together. On my return to New York, I seriously considered becoming a teacher. Now, after 47 years as a lawyer, a return to teaching would provide a certain symmetry to my life.

Perhaps I might teach in a school in India. I have strong emotional ties to India. It was my introduction to foreign travel when I accompanied my mother there one summer to live in New Delhi. She had been invited to teach a course on American foreign policy to Indian graduate students.

We lived in a house at No. 5 Tuglak Lane, the first and only time I have lived in a house. I would travel to the city's center by tonga — a horse-drawn carriage — and return by motorcycle, holding on for dear life to the Sikh driver. Over long weekends, we traveled around the country, including to Kashmir, living on a houseboat on Dall Lake, across from the Shalimar Gardens, in the Himalayas. Teaching in India would be an opportunity for me to work in an extraordinary land.

Perhaps I should do all three — write, teach and travel. ("A traveler," Thoreau wrote, "is to be reverenced as such. His profession is the best symbol of our life. Going from ______ to ______; it is the history of every one of us.")

[2010]

Postscript:

I have chosen to do all three. [2013]

The Red Oak

Making sure no one sees me, I embrace the trunk of my Central Park tree, a red oak planted in the 1920s on the East Green, just inside the park from 70th Street and Fifth Avenue. It is "mine" because the tree has been endowed in my name by board members of Volunteers of Legal Service on the occasion of my retirement as executive director.

No better gift could have been chosen, for Central Park has played a major role in my life.

Before embracing my tree, I first had to select it. To help me do so, I meet with Neil Calvanese, vice president of operations for the Central Park Conservancy, who has worked with park trees for the past 30 years, and Hannah Parker, manager of the Conservancy's Tree Trust.

We visit two favorite places of mine in the park, the first just south of the zoo. Years ago, there was a pony track here. Children, including my sister and me, were placed in pony-drawn carts and led around the track by an attendant.

The pony track is long gone, replaced by grass and trees. Most mornings, on my walk from home through the park to the Fifth Avenue subway station at 60th Street, I sit on a bench here to write. A tranquil, productive way to begin the workday.

On this site, in 1995, I arranged for the planting of two southern magnolia trees, FDR's favorite, following my visit to Warm Springs, Georgia, to attend the ceremony commemorating the 50th anniversary of President Franklin D. Roosevelt's death. For a period of months and years, I watched the trees grow and then, alas, wither, succumbing to the city's severe winter weather.

We then go to the East Green. On weekends, over the years, I have spent many hours on the East Green, seated on the grass, leaning against the rough bark of a red oak where I write and read. From here I see the Frick mansion and the facades of Fifth Avenue apartment buildings.

This red oak is a proud, handsome tree, standing 60 feet tall. Its broad canopy has long provided me with beneficial shade. I select the red oak as my tree.

On hot summer days, I will continue to enjoy its shade and listen to the sound of its swaying branches. At night, I will watch fireflies dart around the trunk.

In the fall, I will admire its bright orange leaves. Every other year I will collect the acorns it sheds.

In winter, I will visit my tree as it braves the elements.

The Portuguese writer José Saramago in "Small Memories, A Memoir", describes his father late in life going "from tree to tree in his garden, embracing their trunks and saying goodbye to them, to their friendly shade, to the fruits he will never eat again."

Late in my life, when the end is near, I will do the same.

[2011]

Acknowledgments

Elizabeth Sheehan designed the book text and cover. Her talent, hard work and enthusiasm for the project are deeply appreciated. And thank you Betty Kelly Sargent for introducing me to Liz.

Lindsay Gibbs handled the manuscript with care and diligence.

I am grateful to Karen Artz Ash, David Sherman and Jennifer Carmen of the law firm of Katten Muchin Rosenman for guidance on copyright matters.

And to Stephen Raphael and Ellen Marks who extended hospitality to me at their law firm.

With deep thanks to Stephen Wilder for your guidance throughout this effort. And also to David Cobb Craig.

To Nelson Gutierrez who advised me on the many mysteries of technology and took my photograph for the back cover.

And thanks also to my friends Lyn Chase, Joan Davidson, Lynn Goldberg, Clay Hiles, Jeannette Watson Sanger and Tom Wallace who provided encouragement and excellent advice.

Publication Notes

The essays in this book originally appeared in The Christian Science Monitor (CSM), The New York Times (NYT), New York Law Journal (NYLJ) and Wall Street Journal (WSJ). Essays from the NYLJ and WSJ are reprinted with permission. Some essays have been edited for this book. The titles of essays appearing in each section of the book follow, along with name of publication and publication date.

WALKING

The City My Feet Know Perfectly, CSM, July 6, 1998

Early Mornings in New York, CSM, April 27, 1992

A Doughnut and Art to Start the Day, CSM, September 1, 2006

Walking Warmly Through a City Winter, CSM, February 24, 2000

New York City's Animal Kingdom, Wild and Tame, CSM, April 25, 2002

Savoring the City, Street by Street, CSM, November 28, 2001

A Symphony of City Sounds, CSM, May 11, 2000

In Stride with Thoreau, CSM, April 16, 1987

Manhattan's Straight Streets, NYLJ, April 17, 2008

Directions, CSM, May 3, 2002

I Am Beginning to Notice More About My Own City, CSM, August 12, 1985

I've Walked the World Without Leaving Home, CSM, March 30, 2000

CENTRAL PARK/GRAND CENTRAL TERMINAL

Amid Skyscrapers, I Enjoy a Vast Estate, CSM, July 25, 2005

My Modest Investment Pays Relaxing Dividends, CSM, September 13, 2001

Cycling Through the Centuries on a Bike, CSM, March 27, 1998

Birdwatching, CSM, June 11, 2003

Considering Time, and Time Well Spent, CSM, February 22, 2002

Celebrating the Season With Songs of All Kinds, CSM, May 16, 2001

A Lifetime at Grand Central, CSM, March 15, 1993

Stargazing in Grand Central Terminal, CSM, January 3, 2000

Subway Notes, NYLJ, February 17, 2011

MOTHER/FATHER

From Russia to Radcliffe, CSM, September 2, 1986

A Russian Soul Rooted in New York, CSM, June 12, 1991

Father, NYLJ, June 18, 2009

A Matter of Priorities, CSM, January 15, 1987

EDUCATION

Sounds of School: Bells, Songs and King's English, CSM, August 26, 1999

Blessed by Embracing Two Cultures, CSM, September 11, 2002

Baseball, WSJ, August 10, 1979

My Evolving Relationship with Mr. Westgate, Saint Bernard's School, Spring, 2005

Late Bloomer, CSM, October 29, 1986

The Other Education I Got at Law School, CSM, October 17, 2001

LAWYER/HOMELESS/PRISONERS

Lives Transformed: My Own and Others, NYLJ, June 8, 2011

Scenes of a City's Grandeur and Need, CSM, February 13, 2002

I Think of David, CSM, December 15, 1986

Working at the Finest Masterworks, CSM, March 31, 1982

Potter's Field, NYT, May 25, 1981

The Two Worlds of Rikers Island, NYLJ, October 17, 1984

Fidelio's Hope, and Mine, CSM, November 17, 1986

C.3.3, NYLJ, November 23, 2012

A New Way of Living and Forgiving, NYLJ, July 3, 2007

APARTMENT/OFFICES

A Strong Sense of Place, NYLJ, December, 2010

The Books Pile Up and So Do the Excuses, CSM, July 26, 2006

My Street, NYLJ, 1983

Workday Views of Sky and Street, CSM, May 16, 1991

My Own Super, CSM, January 24, 2000

Ups and Downs, CSM, March 10, 2005

Pictures on the Wall, CSM, May 31, 1983

PERSONAL

Tuxedo, CSM, December 31, 1998

Keys, CSM, November 22, 2000

Shoelaces, CSM, April 25, 2005

Shoe Polish Box, CSM, July 5, 2001

Clothes, CSM, May 2, 2005
Baseball Cap, CSM, August 20, 2003
A Furry Visitor, CSM, May 7, 2003
Being Tall Has Its Shortcomings, CSM, April 20, 2005
Punctuality, CSM, April 1, 1999
A Landlubber Gets a Taste of the Sea, CSM, July 9, 2004
Watching the World Come In, CSM, July 30, 1997
Hear Ye!!! 'King' William Bares His Soul, NYT, July 12, 1975
New York and Venice, NYLJ, August 21, 2008
A Letter Gets the Lights Turned Back On, CSM, December 8, 2005
Practical and Poetic, CSM, June 29, 2001

BASKETBALL/OPERA

The Highest Court, NYLJ, April 15, 2010 & March 15, 2012
A Day of Basketball and Opera, CSM, July 13, 2005
Notes on the Ring, CSM, May 22, 2000
On Stage, Just a Supernumerary, But…, NYT, January 29, 1984

WRITING

Enriching the Script, NYLJ, October 16, 2008
In the Writing Good Things Come, CSM, September 7, 1988
Subway Rider, Writer, CSM, February 26, 1998
For Chekhov, It Was as Easy as Eating Pancakes, CSM, May 9, 2002
The Editor Sends His Regrets, CSM, October 13, 1988
The Best Companion for a Writer, CSM, May 17, 2006

LITERATURE

Literature and Travel, NYLJ Magazine, December 2009
Chekhov by My Desk, NYLJ, February 19, 2009
A Chekhov Bookworm in New York, CSM, June 18, 2003
Thoreau's Path in New York City, CSM, December 23, 1992
Whitman, CSM, March 1, 1990
Thoreau and Whitman Meet in Brooklyn, NYLJ, September 6, 2007
Volume 50, CSM, June 24, 1987 & September 21, 2000
Book Selections of Founding Fathers, NYLJ, February, 2007

PARTING

Timeless Tides in New York City, CSM, July 5, 2000
Retirement Thoughts, NYLJ, June 17, 2010
The Red Oak, NYLJ, August 10, 2011